Warning Signs

By Alan Caruba

Merril Press
Bellevue, Washington

WARNING SIGNS

First Edition.
Published by the Merril Press.

WARNING SIGNS is distributed by Merril Press, P.O. Box 1682, Bellevue, Washington 98009. Additional copies of this book may be ordered from Merril Press at $15.00 each. Phone 425-454-7009

        Library of Congress Cataloging-In-Publication Data

Caruba, Alan.
    Warning Signs / by Alan Caruba-- 1st ed.
        p. cm.
    ISBN 0-936783-35-4 (pbk.)
        1. Political planning. 2. Conservatism. I. Title

    JF1525.P6C37 2003
    320'.6--dc21

                                        2002043230

Author's Preface

To Robert & Rebecca Caruba

The name of my weekly column, "Warning Signs", came quickly to mind when I first sat down to write on topics of concern to me. It seemed to me that what I most wanted to do was to warn readers about the many domestic and international threats to liberty and freedom, to American values and sovereignty.

Over the years of writing *Warning Signs*, my range of concerns reached out to include the Middle East, not the least because of the wake-up call that 9-11 gave everyone. These days, I pretty much write about whatever is on my mind that week.

There is an inherent, internal discipline to writing a weekly column that requires one to sort out what is important, to look at topics that may not be in the headlines, to identify the causes for problems, reveal the people and organizations behind the street theatre that so often accompanies the great issues of our times.

So many of the issues have a hidden agenda. In the past, the villains—Hitler, Stalin, Mao—were easy to identify, but today many hide behind positions advocated by so-called "non-governmental organizations" with noble sounding goals, all of which end up as being a quest for absolute power over the lives of free people or greater control over those who are not free.

The problem is exacerbated by the often unbelievable and lamentable ignorance people have regarding the past, whether it be World War II, the Civil War, or any other epic of history in which battles were fought to protect hard-gained freedoms. The public's general lack of knowledge about science is also exploited to frighten them with endless scary scenarios. This is why I have also written about education issues. Those who control the education of a nation's children influence their ability to make informed decisions about its future as they mature into adults. Education today is about indoctrination, about attitudes, about feeling good instead of feeling challenged to learn, to succeed.

I have been greatly helped over the years by men and women who are experts in their own fields. The facts offered are all documented by vast files of articles I have maintained for many years and by a huge library, thanks to more than four decades of having been a book reviewer.

I am very fond of facts. They are hard to refute. That said, I also am fond of expressing my opinion, based on those facts. That others may interpret the same facts differently is a given. They will and they do. In America, they have the freedom to do so.

This is a book that will mostly please people whose political choice is conservatism. For most of my life I was a liberal. I was raised in a home where Franklin D. Roosevelt was a demigod, where the United Nations was going to save the world from the scourge of war, where the Democrats were intended to run the nation forever. Vietnam changed my thinking about the political leadership that was being offered. It was not, however, until Ronald Reagan brought about the downfall of the Soviet Union that my thinking began to change significantly. Eight years of Bill and Hillary Clinton confirmed my worst fears.

One could say that I was liberated from being a liberal. This is not an uncommon experience. Many in their youth embrace liberalism as the gateway to a better, if utopian, world. With age, experience and knowledge, one comes to understand that freedom is always under siege and must be defended on a daily basis.

In 1990, after years of writing for various publications about issues involving the stranglehold that environmentalism had imposed on the nation, I founded The National Anxiety Center © as a clearinghouse for information about "scare campaigns" designed to influence public opinion and policy. These campaigns all have one thing in common, they are built on lies and deception.

I had seen how the Greens had waged a relentless war against pesticides and herbicides, beneficial chemicals that literally protect human life against the diseases and the damage done by insect and rodent pests, and the destruction of the crops that feed not just Americans, but millions around the world.

iv

I was aware, too, that "global warming" had followed a campaign by the Greens in the 1970s warning people about "a coming Ice Age." Having failed to frighten enough people with that lie, the Greens reversed themselves and began perpetrating the greatest hoax of modern times.

The Center became my vehicle to comment on so many Green programs that always seemed aimed at either harming the economy and/or gaining control over people's lives. That's why the title "Warning Signs" for the columns and now for this book is so appropriate.

I hope you enjoy this collection of commentaries written and posted on the web site of The National Anxiety Center at www.anxietycenter.com. If you do, e-mail me at acaruba@aol.com or write to me care of The National Anxiety Center at 9 Brookside Road, Maplewood, NJ 07040.

Acknowledgements

There are many people who should be acknowledged for their support over the years, helping me get my message out. Those mentioned below are far outnumbered by the many friends and colleagues whose names do not appear, but who know who they are and how appreciated they are.

I start with my friend, Paul Driessen, polemist extraordinaire, who suggested the publication of this book to Ron Arnold of the Free Enterprise Institute and Alan Gottlieb of Merril Press.

I owe a debt of gratitude to my friend, Tom DeWeese, the President of the American Policy Center, a think tank devoted to the most basic values of this nation. He is one of my heroes who is always on the front lines defending our freedom and liberties. His encouragement has been beyond measure.

Thanks, too, go to Scott Hogenson, Executive Editor of CNSNews.Com, whose invaluable web site provides the news that cannot be found in the liberal mainstream press that informed citizens need each to address the issues of concern and the commentaries including my own to understand them better.

I have been very fortunate to have the friendship and support of many Internet editors who share my writings with the visitors to their sites. They include A.J. Toogood, editor of the Toogood Report; Steve Martinovich editor of EnterStageRight.Com; J.J. Johnson, editor of SierraTimes.Com; Lewis J. Goldberg, editor of Patriotist.Com; Bill Rayment, editor of ConservativeMonitor.Com; Bill Mayer, editor of PipeBombNews.Com; Brent Barksdale, editor of PoliticalUSA.Com: Tom

Barratt, editor of OpinionNet.Com; Erik Barath, editor of NewsFilter.Org; Phil Brennan, editor of Wednesday on the Web; Don Hundt, editor of Let Freedom Ring; Brad Ullrich, editor of Off-Road.Com; Paul Walter, editor of NewsWithViews.Com; Mark DaCunha, editor of Capitalism Magazine.Com; Lionel Waxman, editor of Waxman Media's Flashpoint; Don Holtzinger, editor of Thought You Should Know; James J. McGrody, editor of TexasPlainTalk.Com; Jim Sesi, editor of MichNews.Com; and Kevin Burt, editor of the CheyenneNetwork.Com.

Thanks are due to the expertise and shared wisdom of my friend, Henry Lamb, the editor of *Eco-Logic*. His encyclopedic knowledge about the United Nations has been invaluable. Steve Milloy of JunkScience.Com has been an inspiration and Charlotte Thompson Iserbyt, fighting to save our nation's educational system, deserves my thanks and admiration.

Contents

Warning Signs

By Alan Caruba

The Evil of Environmentalism

In the commentaries that follow, I hope you will discern the pattern that is well known to those of us who have closely examined the environmental movement. It is utterly totalitarian in its intent. It uses deception to achieve its goal of global power and that deception is primarily intended to frighten people to accept its programs to "save the Earth."

As I say repeatedly in my commentaries, the Earth is 4.5 billion years old. It does not need saving because humans have very little real impact on it. Here in the United States of America, if you added all the land occupied by cities and suburbs, highways and roadways, airports and seaports, the sum total would be around 3 percent of the entire landmass of the nation. Most of the Earth has little or no human population because humans tend to congregate in towns, villages and, of course, in vast cities. Most of the time, these cities exist near major oceans or waterways.

Humans have been around for about 10,000 years, following the last Ice Age, and have evolved civilizations for only the past 5,000. True, there are a lot of humans around these days, but that is precisely because the inventions, the innovations, and the advances of mankind have permitted this burst of human population. The struggle in which we find ourselves engaged is between those who believe humanity is a good thing and those who believe it is a "cancer" on the Earth to be exterminated.

No single economic theory has killed more people than Communism. That includes the millions killed by the Nazis in World War II—that evil regime was made up of National *Socialists* who patterned themselves after the Soviets—and the emergence of Red China that killed millions more.

1

If the world and humanity is to survive this monstrous ideology, Capitalism, free trade, and the rule of law must succeed and, with it, so must the spread of freedom where individuals can elect their representatives to govern.

Environmentalism is simply the façade of Communism. It is the Socialist magician's slights of hand, making you think the ball is in his right hand when it is in his left one. It is pure deception. Its goal is to enslave you.

Greens Reveal their Plan for Global Domination

On March 14, 2002, a program to capture the Capitalist system and control it for the purpose of advancing the twisted values of environmentalism was spelled out in a presentation titled "Restructuring the Global Economy."

According to the Greens behind this plan, "Economic globalization is the greatest single contributor to the massive ecological crisis of our time, yet this is an aspect that is often ignored by the media, NGOs, policymakers, and citizens. Its inherent emphasis on increased trade requires corresponding expansion of transportation of infrastructures, airports, seaports, roads, rail-lines, pipelines, dams, electric grids, many of these are constructed in pristine landscapes, often on indigenous people's lands."

"Increased transport also uses drastically increased fossil fuels, adding to the problems of climate change, ozone depletion, and ocean, air, and soil pollution."

There is a very big problem with the assertion quoted above. None of it is true. If the U.S., let alone the rest of the world, did not have airports, seaports, roads, rail-lines, pipelines, dams and electric grids, you would not be reading this, nor would there be too many goods in your local supermarket or mall.

Nor is the world running out of so-called "fossil fuels." Moreover, world trade is generally seen as the best way to lift Third World nations out of their grinding poverty while increasing peaceful and fruitful relations between industrialized nations. More goods mean more money and more jobs everywhere in a world that has six billion mouths to feed every day.

At the heart of the environmental—Green—movement have been people who are hardcore Marxists, haters of Capitalism and the corporations and countless small businesses that sustain it. Their problem, however, is that Communism doesn't work. It has a record of enslaving and killing millions of people who fell under its control.

To Randall Hayes, the man who presented his paper at the 2002 Johns Hopkins Symposium on Foreign Affairs, Capitalism "is an absurd economic system rapidly destroying nature, cultural diversity, and decent local life." Admitting that there were no "attractive alternatives" to Capitalism, he offered proposal that it "be radically improved, humanized, and ecologized."

The key word here is "radically." Humanity is not high on the list of priorities for the Greens who thrive on programs that kill large numbers of people deprived of pesticides to protect them against Nature's greatest vectors of disease, insect and rodent pests. Deprive farmers of the pesticides and herbicides needed to protect their crops against these predators. Deprive people of electrical power from non-polluting hydroelectric dams or nuclear utilities and they remain impoverished. And, most importantly, deprive people of a voice in their affairs through democratic elections by destroying the sovereignty of nations.

The other key word is "ecologized" and that, presumably, means substituting the lies and other control mechanisms that would render what's left of Capitalism the tool of a single group of un-elected Green elites operating under the aegis of the United Nations.

Who is Randall Hayes? He is the president of the radical Rainforest Action Network. He has created the International Forum on Globalization IFOG), described by Ron Arnold, the author of *Undue Influence, Trashing the Economy* and several other books on the Greens, as "assortment of some 60 anti-capitalist organizations and intellectuals from 25 nations." These groups and others have been patiently and malevolently putting together a plan for global domination for decades. The operating element of the plan is the United Nations which, itself, has made it clear it intends to be the sole global government for the entire planet.

Up to now, however, no Green has so boldly stated the true intention of the movement. The plan would dismantle the institutions that monitor global trade and substitute UN agencies in their place. They claim to be driven by the desire to save the Earth and the basis for their claims are the totally bogus "global warming" hoax and others that assert that the air, the water, the soil, and all life on Earth is either polluted or endangered. The Earth is 4.5 billion years old. It does not need saving, particularly if that means the enslavement of the human race.

What Hayes and his fellow Greens claim is hogwash! Every advance in science and technology has come from learning how to secure the maximum benefit of Earth's natural resources.

Do not take it for granted you can place a call to a friend in Europe or Australia and hear them as clearly as if they lived next door. Do not take for granted that the water from your faucet is potable. Do not take for granted your supermarket will be filled with a huge variety of foods, products to keep your home clean, and other items, all of which arrived by truck. Do not take for granted that public health mosquito control programs protect you against West Nile Virus or Malaria. Do not take for granted you will be permitted to get in your car or get on a plane to go anywhere you want.

Nothing in modern life exists without the research and development that has extended your life. It has been entrepreneurs and corporations who have risked huge sums to bring about progress.

The Greens hate progress.

In this, they are financially supported by foundations whose goal it is to control the world's money supply and, thereby, its future. They include the Rockefeller Brothers Fund, the MacArthur Foundation, the Ford Foundation, HKH Foundation and the Turner Foundation, among just a few of those funding IFOG. All fund anti-globalization groups.

As Ron Arnold points out, Randall Hayes' Rainforest Action Network is "a shakedown operation, as RAN's arrest record indicates. He doesn't mention that his organization used unlawful activities such as trespass, intimidation and vandalism against his targets." Indeed, the Internal Revenue Service "has been asked to revoke RAN's tax exempt status for very offenses."

The IFOG plan that Hayes unveiled is a plan to rule the world. All despotisms proudly announce their plans. Had the world read and acted upon the rantings of Adolph Hitler's *Mein Kampf* in the 1930s, we would have been spared World War II. Had the world acted to thwart the aims of the *Communist Manifesto*, Russia would have been spared seventy years of horror and Red China would not now be threatening the United States with ICBMs.

Hayes' plan would give non-profit groups access to the most radical economic decision-making power within the United Nations. It would remove corporations and nations from that process. It would impose restrictions on the use of all natural resources and it would do so in the name of saving the Earth. From whom? From YOU!

Environmental Corruption: A Cascade of Lies

Dennis T. Avery, a senior fellow for the Hudson Institute and a former senior policy analyst for the U.S. Department of State, recently took note of sanctions applied to Steven R. Arnold, a former researcher at the Tulane University Center for Bioenvironmental Research. The Federal Office of Research Integrity found that Arnold had "committed scientific misconduct by intentionally falsifying the research results published in the *Journal Science* and by providing falsified and fabricated materials to investigating officials."

His punishment? He will be unable to receive federal research funding for five years. Avery called it "one of the most dramatic scientific frauds of modern times," noting that the Tulane Center said it found that various pesticides, safe when tested individually, were 1,000 times more dangerous when tested together. It raised the specter of modern agriculture's chemicals undermining the health of the human population and the natural ecology through a blind spot in our regulatory testing." And it was a lie.

This is part of the campaign of endless lies designed to secure the ban of every single pesticide and herbicide that protects human health against insect and rodent predators, and the vast food crops produced by American farmers. In 1996 a book was published, *Our Stolen Future: Are We Threatening Our Fertility, Intelligence and Survival? – A Scientific Detective Story*. Written by Theo Colbert, even the author her book admitted it was based on mere suspicions. It has been cited, however, as proof of yet another bogus threat conjured up by environmentalists."

"The book speculated that man-made chemicals were causing ailments ranging from cancer to attention deficit disorder by disrupting our endocrine systems," noted Avery. The book's forward was written by then Vice President Al Gore. When Arnold's falsified research was published in 1996, Carol Browner, the Administrator of the Environmental Protection

5

Agency, said, "The new study is the strongest evidence to date that combinations of estrogenic materials may be potent enough to significantly increase the risk of breast cancer, prostate cancer, birth defects and other major health concerns."

As we now know, there is no such evidence, except that purposely created to further the goal of the environmental movement to end the use of pesticides and herbicides. Beginning with Rachel Carson's bogus and discredited "science" in *Silent Spring*, this attack on beneficial chemicals has never ceased.

In a similar fashion, Michael Bellesile's book, *Arming America* was seized upon by gun-control advocates as having demolished "the myth" that individuals have the right to gun ownership. The book asserted that private gun ownership was uncommon in early America. It turns out that the author deliberately misinterpreted Colonial documents, misquoted early federal laws, distorted historical accounts, and cited San Francisco records that experts agree were destroyed in the 1906 earthquake.

The willingness to lie regarding environmental issues was revealed in December when it was found that federal and state wildlife biologists had planted false evidence of a rare cat species in two national forests, the Gifford Pinchot National Forest and Wenatchee National Forest in Washington State. This is the same forest area that the Earth Liberation Front has recently boasted of "spiking" trees in order to do injury to lumberjacks culling trees for purposes of forest management.

Now comes another report of "bio-fraud" where a Washington State fish and wildlife biologist is alleged to have asked a taxidermist for grizzly bear hair samples in March of last year. The use of such hair samples could have been used to taint a study of grizzly bear habitat, ultimately affecting recreation, timber, mining, road construction and other uses of throughout the State. Officials are beginning to wonder just how much of this kind of deliberate deception has been at work at the state and federal level to achieve the environmental goals of shutting down essential industries and the recreational use of public lands. One is reminded of the "Spotted Owl" hoax that devastated the timber industry throughout the Pacific Northwest.

The cascade of lies about everything environmental should, by now, have convinced the public that U.S. government officials responsible for setting national policies and environmental groups seeking to determine what those policies should be cannot be trusted. The public, however, has rarely paid any attention to anything than the lies published by a compliant and complacent mainstream media that has fully adopted the goals of the environmental and animal rights movements.

The costs of these policies are astronomical. Billions of dollars are wasted on wasteful programs said to "protect" the environment. Billions of dollars are going to be allocated to States and environmental groups to put more and more land aside from any use. Late on the evening of December 20th, the Senate, without any public debate or a recall vote, passed S-990, The American Wildlife Enhancement Act of 2001. We will never know who voted for this act. This was the same tactic used to pass the UN Convention on Desertification. Now $600 million in taxpayer dollars will be given out for "the acquisition of an area of land or water that is suitable or capable of being made suitable for feeding, resting or breeding by wildlife." Translation: Any property can be designated for virtual seizure. One can only pray the President will veto this full-scale attack on property rights in America.

This is how environmental groups achieve their goals. They are goals based in a consuming hatred of humankind and its need for food and shelter. They are goals that are intended to undermine and destroy America's economic power, based on access to its vast natural resources. They are goals intended to strip Americans of the most fundamental right of self-defense. They are the goals of those who believe they are morally superior to you and I, and therefore have the right to subvert the truth to achieve total control over our lives and our nation.

While Americans look to the Middle East and elsewhere, fearful of terrorist organizations intent on harming our lives and our society, they continue to ignore the internal enemies who, by stealth and deception, work to destroy the progress of real science that protects and extends our lives, and to undermine our most fundamental Constitutional protections.

If we lose this struggle, it will be because of our inertia and indifference. The environmentalists, animal rights, and gun control advocates are counting on that.

Air Pollution Lies

An interesting juxtaposition of news stories appeared in the November 11, 1999 issue of *USA Today*. They say a lot about the way the public is continually misled about air pollution. "Panel flags 80 million pounds in pollutant leaks" was the headline in Traci Wilson's article about a report by the minority, i.e., Democratic, staff of the House Committee on Government Reform.

The report estimated that 80 million pounds of volatile organic compounds (VOCs) leak unreported from oil refineries every year. Now, bear in mind, that any source of fossil fuel energy, oil and coal, has long been the target of the Greens.

Reading further, however, there was a story out of Cotalo, Ecuador, about two volcanoes spewing ash plumes and showers of red-hot rocks, a signal that they are ready to blow big-time. The last time Tungurahua erupted in 1916, it kept it up for two years. Guagua Pichincha's last major eruption was in 1660. In Antarctica, there's an active volcano, Mount Erebus, that accounts for the thinning of ozone right over where it is spewing forth tons of gases. They don't tell you that every time they report on an ozone "hole" there.

Now for a little perspective on air pollution. In 1991, Mount Pinatubo on the island of Luzon in the Philippines erupted after nearly 600 years of dormancy. The eruption blew nearly 500 feet off the volcano and into the stratosphere. *The eruption sent nearly 20 million tons of sulfur dioxide gas into the surrounding atmosphere*. The ash particles landed as far away as the United States.

There are hundreds of volcanoes throughout the world, many are active, and some of them are in the oceans. The Ecuadorian volcanoes will release millions of *tons* of gas and ash. And the Greens in your government are all worked up over a few million *pounds* of VOCs which they "estimate" to result from refinery operations. This is bogus!

The earth "leaks" tons of natural gases every year. That's how it works! The Greens, as usual, are conning you and everyone else about man-made VOCs. Can they be reduced? Probably. Should huge fines be imposed on refineries, utilities, and others to achieve this? Should more and more demands be made on auto manufacturers? Should more intensive auto inspections be imposed on motorists? No! We're already making great progress toward clean air under existing laws.

This is not about clean air. It's about forcing up the costs of energy and transportation for everyone. The Greens want to punish us for driving to work or picking up the kids from school. The Greens want to punish us for pumping oil out of the earth and digging up coal. They're nuts. And they are liars.

"Protecting" U.S. Forests by Burning Them

Dramatic video of the loss of a fire-fighting airplane has driven home the danger that forest fires represent. In California, Colorado, and other States, homeowners are seeing them go up in flames as the beginning of yet another spate of cataclysmic forest fires occurs again. The reason the U.S. is experiencing these fires can be found in the policies of environmental groups crying out to protect "wilderness" and its own Forest Service that is carrying out an environmental agenda.

You protect forests by providing for their proper management, and that means timber companies have to come in and thin the old and diseased trees. Overgrown brush has to be removed as well. The U.S. timber industry has been systematically attacked by environmentalists for decades in the name of "protecting" our forests. Remember the "Spotted Owl" hoax that claimed they were "endangered" and, in the process, led to vast acres of Northwest forests being put off limits to any use?

They are still at it. The U.S. Public Interest Research Group, a Ralph Nader organization, along with the Southern Appalachian Forest Coalition, and the Sierra Club are demanding that the Bush Administration "keep its word to protect 58.8 million acres of national forest lands." They are pushing hard for legislation that codifies the "Roadless Area Conservation Rule" which they describe as "one of the most sweeping land conservation measures in decades."

It is a completely idiotic proposal. It is criminally stupid. You cannot fight forest fires if there are no roads with which to reach the areas going up in smoke. "Conservation", however, in Green-Talk means putting land aside so that no one can use it for any reason.

The Federal District Court in Idaho has placed an injunction on the implementation of this "roadless" rule that was developed in secret by the Clinton Administration and the Heritage Forests Campaign to deny access to 58 million acres of forestland that is the property of all Americans. On June 5th, forty-four members of the House of Representatives wrote to President Bush urging him to resist any effort to enact the "roadless" rule.

Americans have been led to believe we are losing all our forests at a time when many forests are expanding. The United States is still home to 70 percent of the forestland that was here in 1600, fully 747 million acres! Of these, 247 million acres (33.5 percent) are reserved from harvest by law or represent slow-growing woodlands unsuitable for timber productions.

There are 490 million acres called timberlands, forests that can produce more than 20 cubic feet of wood per acre annually. The total amount of large-tree standing timber in the U.S. has increased by 30 percent since 1950. U.S. forestlands covered 732 million acres in 1920; today they cover 747 million acres.

The Greens, however, have set about finding ways to put these productive and incredibly valuable forestlands aside so that neither the timber industry, nor anyone else can use them. This explains why the cost of building a new home or making an addition to an existing one has risen by an average of anywhere between a thousand and five thousand dollars. It's not that we don't have the wood! It's that the Greens will not let the timber industry access it. It is nuts that the U.S. is actually importing wood from Canada!

"Preserving and protecting our national forests for future generations must remain a priority," said Tennessee Congressman Bob Clement, as he sought support for the "roadless" legislation. Give me a break. We've got tons of national forests. In fact, our national forests were set aside with language that specifically made it clear that they were for the benefit of Americans, including their full use for recreation and for timber. This is just another Green plot to deny Americans access to and use of their natural wonders and natural resources.

If this "roadless" idiocy doesn't get the job done for the Greens, there's always the "Heritage Areas Act", (H.R. 2388) an equally hideous piece of legislation that was just voted out of the House Resources Committee. It would simplify the process for establishing "Heritage Areas" which is the federal government's way of grabbing more and more land while denying Americans access to it. The Greens would turn the whole nation into a picture postcard to look at, but a place where no one can use to fish, hunt, camp, hike, visit with a snowmobile or off-track vehicle of any kind.

What you are never told is that half the land of the twelve westernmost States is actually owned by the Federal government. Federal lands comprise 86 percent of Nevada, 68 percent of Alaska, 64 percent of Utah, and 44 percent of California. The big lie is that "urban sprawl" is destroying the wilderness, but the total amount of land of U.S. cities, suburbs, highways, bridges and other structures adds up to a paltry 3 percent of the entire landmass.

Meanwhile, one day you will wake up and find that your home, farm or business is now in a newly declared "Heritage Area" that nobody bothered to tell you about. Then the government takes it away from you because it's ruining the view.

This nation, this America, is being stolen from us, acre by acre, as part of the Green agenda and because there are legislators who want to add to the 40 percent of the nation already owned by the Federal Government. You want to visit a place where the government owns all the land? Visit Cuba, Vietnam or Red China.

Greens Attack the U.S. Military

As America mobilizes to win the war against terrorism, the quality and capability of our Armed Forces is going to be an important priority. Throughout the years of the Clinton-Gore Administration, following the Gulf War, the destruction of our military was the priority. Helping in that process were the faceless bureaucrats, many still in place, pledged to environmentalism at any cost.

"Endangered species has power to halt war training" was the headline on an article in an October 2000 edition of the *Washington Times*. Written by Steve Miller and datelined Fort Irwin, California, the article began "What may be one of the most formidable threats to national security today has a craggy face, scaly arms and, well, he likes a little grass now and then." He was referring to the desert tortoise.

Soldiers on the Army training center's battlefield were instructed to call a commander if a desert tortoise crawled out of a hole. At that point, the entire training exercise would stop. This insanity has been repeated on every military base in the nation in one fashion or another.

11

The U.S. Defense Department oversees and controls 17 million acres of U.S. land, down from 30 million acres after World War II. It has been losing the fight for space to train a modern military for years. When asked about the need for national security, a spokesman for the Bureau of Land Management (the same one that shut off water to the farmers of Klamath Valley) was quoted in the article as saying, "It is not in our purview to make a determination related to national security. Ours is to make sure the Endangered Species Act is complied with."

There are hundreds of federal employees throughout its many agencies who are little more than covert agents for the environmental movement. Their concern is not for national security, but for the security of an endangered species or some other environmental mandate that makes it impossible to train and equip our military to protect our nation at home and on foreign shores. They are what, during WWII, was called "a Fifth Column."

There are also many elected members of Congress such as Rep. Bob Filner, a Democrat from the 50th District of California, the San Diego area, now in his fifth term. This is a district where you will find a large contingent of U.S. Navy ships, part of our Pacific Fleet. You will also find the Space and Naval Warfare Systems Center and Naval Air Force there. In June, this moron introduced the Military Environmental Responsibility Act (H.R. 2154) that seeks to remove all military exemptions from existing environmental, worker, and public safety laws and regulations. His bill, presumably doomed, would have put every element of our military under the thumb of the Environmental Protection Agency! The California delegation in Congress is so shot through with Socialists and other enemies of this nation, it constitutes an invading army in its own right.

The national and international environmental movement—the Greens—has been engaged in undermining the U.S. military for years. Few have taken notice of it. The Greens represent an instrument of foreign and domestic Socialist agendas, all of which are aimed at undermining this nation's economic viability, its sovereignty, and its military strength and readiness.

One of the most egregious examples has been the campaign to force the U.S. military to switch from lead-based ammunition to that requiring tungsten. This "Green ammo" was said to be necessary because of the "environmental threat" of lead bullets and other shells. The bullets fired from standard issue M-16 rifles have always been made of lead, as was virtually every other bullet ever fired by our military going back to the days of the American Revolution.

The Green mandate for tungsten bullets ignored the fact that this metal costs vastly more than lead, easily twice as much. It also ignored the fact that the greatest source of this metal is Red China. For several years now, the United States Army has been testing and considering the overhaul of its ammunition under intense pressure from the Greens within the Clinton-Gore Administration.

In 1999, Rep. Duncan Hunter (R-CA) pointed out that "The Clinton-Gore team has bled the military such that the Army is short $3.5 billion worth of basic ammunition alone." He reported that the combined shortages for Marines, Navy and Air Force had caused "critical shortages of spare parts, equipment and training." At the time he was saying this, some 11,000 military personnel were on food stamps! Mission capability rates, barely two years ago, had fallen below 70 percent across the boards for all services.

In May 2000, *Insight* magazine published an article, "The Greening of the Military" by Catherine Edwards that should have initiated hearings in Congress and calls for the total rejection of the way environmentalists have undermined the military. It noted that a report by the Cato Institute, issued on the eve of Earth Day, warned that there was "a high risk that efforts by the Clinton Administration to turn environmental issues into a national-security concern will result in the militarization of environmental policy."

In 1993, under then-Secretary of Defense, Les Aspin, an Office of Deputy Undersecretary of Defense for Environmental Security was created. Its mission was to address issues such as "environmental degradation and the role of the military." The only thing the military is supposed to degrade is the enemy's ability to wage war.

A former environmental lawyer, Sherri Goodman, has run the office. As recently as last year, the office was bragging about protecting the environment of military personnel and their families, despite the fact that many bases have long since fallen into disrepair. Her office pushed for "environmentally sound technology and management programs within the Department of Defense." It actually claimed that, behind the threat of weapons of mass destruction and terrorism, were "environmental factors."

What has occurred, in reality, is the diversion of U.S. military personnel to undertake environmental projects that have nothing to do with the security of the United States or our fighting forces stationed overseas.

The Green attack on our military includes a propaganda campaign, as does all environmentalism. One example is *America's Defense Monitor,* a weekly television series broadcast on an estimated 65 Public Broadcasting

System outlets and cable stations. If you visit their website (cdi.org) you can order videos of anti-nuclear programs such as *Radioactive America*, *The Military-Industrial Squeeze*, and *Dark Cloud: Our Strange Love Affair with the Bomb*.

One ADM program is entitled An *Environmental Industrial Complex*? This program argues *against* ballistic missile systems, fighter planes, and new submarines, suggesting the spending the money on solving environmental problems would be better. All of their programs are intended to convince viewers to believe that way too much money is being spent on our military. Among the experts appearing on it are Penelope Hanson, director of the Environmental Protection Agency's Environmental Technology Verification Program and Jim MacKenzie, a senior associate with the World Resources Institute.

In just the few ways enumerated here, we can see how, once again, the Greens have infiltrated our military establishment, just as they have done in our nation's schools, and throughout federal and state government agencies. In every case, they have instituted and supported programs that will continue to have serious consequences for our national security and sovereignty.

It is time to identify and root out these enemies of our military. A good first step would be to rescind the DOD Office of Environmental Security. This would help to begin restoring our nation's ability to wage war effectively against its enemies at home and abroad. After that will come the rescinding of most of the nearly one third of all Federal laws and regulations that have been imposed in the name of "protecting the environment."

Condors Galore!

(October 1999)

I have always been opposed to the Endangered Species Act and the nonsense surrounding the whole question of whether we can or even should "save" any species. Every time we've gotten involved, the result has always turned out to be something else than intended.

Take for example, the $20 million effort to save a damned vulture, the condor. These creatures have a wingspan that can be nine and a half feet across, a life span of 40 to 50 years, and your money has been spent to insure they do not vanish from the skies. Lately, whole bunches of them have been showing up in Pine Mountain Club, a community about fifty miles northwest of Los Angeles. Some of the locals are less than thrilled.

The U.S. Fish and Wildlife Service coordinator of the condor breeding program, Robert Mesta,was quoted as saying that it remained to be seen whether the condors bred in captivity would be different from those that were captured. Well, duh! "These guys are going to have to learn to be wild condors, he said. Wrong! You're wild if you're born in the wild and raised in the wild by a real life momma condor, but absent that, you are going to hanker for the company of humans, just like the Condor Convention being held in Pine Mountain Club.

Now, I have never bought into this nonsense that every species is going extinct. The simple fact is that Nature keeps tabs on these things. When the U.S. government does, you get a situation like the one in August 1998 when the USFWS announced it was removing 33 species from the endangered species list, bringing its total of "saved" species to 60.

Turns out that 12 were delisted due to extinction, a natural process last time I checked. Another 24 were delisted because of "data errors." That's bureaucratic talk for having been under-counted in the first place and thus they were *never* endangered. Then there were 9 species that exist solely on federal lands and thus are protected without the ESA. There were three species deemed to have recovered due to the ban on DDT, but if you download the excellent study on DDT available from Junkscience.Com, you will discover this ain't necessarily so. Finally, the 12 remaining species were conserved through the efforts of state agencies and private organizations with only a minimal contribution by the federal government.

In short, the big USFWS announcement was just a tissue of lies. Only EIGHT out of the more than 1,400 listed species have recovered since the act was passed in 1973. The millions spent in the years since then have been a waste! The economic losses incurred by private property owners since then are incalculable.

Lately we're told that salmon need to be protected. Well, a variety of marine mammals that *eat salmon* have been protected and, as their population has grown, they have been eating a lot of salmon. Then there are all the problems that have occurred since the program to re-introduce wolves into areas populated by ranchers and their herds has led to a world of trouble for both. The California ban on hunting cougars has put the bighorn sheep in jeopardy, a virtual death warrant for these magnificent creatures. A developer in New Jersey was told he couldn't build needed housing because the timber rattlesnake is on the State's endangered list! That's just what we need in this populous State, more rattlesnakes. And let's not forget the effort to preserve the black bears. We definitely need more black bears in suburban New Jersey.

Meanwhile, throughout the northeast and other sections of the nation, there are so many protected Canadian geese they have overrun parks, golf courses, and other facilities intended for human use. Don't even talk about deer. There are so many of them in the suburbs that people are going nuts as they eat their beloved flowers, expensive hedges, and everything else that takes their fancy. Afraid of humans? Not a bit.

Let's tell the truth about the Endangered Species Act. It exists as just one more device the Greens use to stall any kind of development anywhere, whether it's a Delhi Sand Fly in Nevada used to stop the building of a hospital or rattlesnakes to stop new housing in the Garden State. It is not about protecting endangered species. It is another way to slow needed facilities for humans and attack whole enterprises like the timber industry, the fishing industry, and ranchers nationwide. For the best information on the ESA, visit the National Wilderness Institute at www.nwi.org/home.org.

What's the lesson we should draw from this nonsense? It's time to eliminate the Endangered Species Act and let Mother Nature do what she does best, sort out those that will join the other 95 percent of all the species that ever lived on earth that are extinct.

Ending Famine Forever: Genetically Modified Foods

One of the Four Horsemen of the Apocalypse, along with Disease and War, is Famine. For the relatively short history of man on earth, famine has killed millions and continues to do so today. We who routinely wander the aisles of the modern supermarket, deciding which of the twenty brands and styles of bread we want to eat, having a insanely huge choice of breakfast cereals, strolling past refrigerated cases of every kind of frozen food imaginable, and browsing through the selection of fresh meats and fishes, can hardly imagine what famine is.

All this took a while to evolve. Around 8,000 BC, agriculture-based societies began to develop in Europe and Asia. People began to save the best seed from their harvest to plant the following season. Some seeds did better than others in various kinds of soils and under various kinds of weather conditions. People noticed that. By selecting certain seeds over others, they were genetically engineering a better crop. They didn't know it that of course, nor could they have imagined a world in which these two words, *genetically engineering* or *genetically modifying*, would be used to stop the greatest advance in agriculture in 10,000 years.

By 1800 BC, yeast was being used to make wine, beer and leavened bread. This was the first use of microorganisms to create new types of food. Quite possibly, some people were frightened by this new invention, until, of course, they began to taste the wine, beer and bread.

Let us now leap forward in time. It was not until 1795 that Nicolas-Francois Appert invented a way to preserve fresh foods by heating and sealing it in metal or glass containers. The reason he came up with this was that Napoleon needed a way to feed his troops so they could ravage Europe and attack Russia. He offered a big reward to anyone who could devise a way to provide fresh, safe food. Thus began the canned food industry!

In 1856, Louis Pasteur invented a process of heating liquids to destroy harmful or unwanted organisms, germs that killed people. It was a huge leap forward in food safety. That was less than 150 years ago. In 1865, an Austrian botanist, Gregor Mendel conducted experiments on pea plants in a monastery garden, concluding that something unseen was passing traits from one generation of peas to another. His findings would be ignored for several decades. He had begun the science of genetics between morning and evening prayers.

Now, let's get to the more recent century. In 1914, Clarence Birdseye invented quick-frozen foods, making many seasonal vegetables, meats and fish available at any time of the year. Some people probably were frightened of the idea of defrosting these foods and actually eating them. People tend to be afraid of new ideas.

In 1953, James Watson and Francis Crick, two researchers, defined the structure of DNA, leading to a better understanding of how cells in all living things store, duplicate, and pass on genetic material from generation to generation. Within the lifetime of a single person, we had moved from Mendel to cracking the DNA code. By 1990, the U.S. Department of Agriculture had approved the first food product modified by biotechnology, Chymogen, an enzyme used in place of rennet in cheesemaking.

17

Alan Caruba

On January 22, 2000, more than six hundred scientists from around the world signed a "Declaration in Support of Agricultural Biotechnology" because just about every environmental organization you can name was busy trying to put an end to the use of this new technology which can feed the planet's population of six billion people. Not only that, it can feed them without having to cut down a single tree to create new farmland. It gets better; it can do it while reducing the need for pesticides to combat thousands of pests that attack food crops.

Now, I ask you, if the Greens are so hell-bent to save the earth, why are they so completely lined up against saving a few million lives that could benefit from something called food! The answer is that the Greens always have and always will oppose anything that benefits human beings. They will save the whales, the wolves and the grizzly bears. They will burn down ski resorts to save the bobcat, they will attack the right of ranchers to graze their cattle or sheep on federal land. They will get the key chemical for refrigeration and air conditioning banned. They will seek to ban every pesticide and herbicide needed to protect against disease and the growing of crops, but the one thing they will *NOT* do is anything that will improve and protect the lives of human beings!

Farmers have been genetically modifying crop plants for centuries, using hybridization and selection techniques, but when modern science can enhance food crops to grow more on less land, with less use of chemicals, and to be more nutritious, the Greens were in the streets of Seattle trying to stop it.

Throughout Europe, the effort is on to ban the import of GM foods. Here in the United States, legislation requiring that GM products be labeled has been introduced in Congress. Some major corporations have already caved into the Greenpeace demands that they not purchase GM crops in the manufacture of their food products. In Lansing, Michigan, a visiting associate professor had her office set on fire by radical environmentalists on New Year's Eve because she is engaged in research to increase food production and making food more nutritious.

Do you see a pattern here? The only people that want to insure that Famine remains one of the Four Horsemen of the Apocalypse are the Greens.

Are Humans Using Up Too Much Sun?

"The energy of the sun, captured by plants and passed on to animals, powers everything in our world—dolphins leaping out of the ocean, geese moving across the sky, people stirring their morning oatmeal."

So says Elizabeth Sawin. Her article, published in *Grist* Magazine, was entitled "There Goes the Sun: humans are gobbling up too much of the sun's energy."

Now, if this strikes you as too stupid to deserve comment, you're right. On the other hand, I will comment on it because it reflects what lots and lots and lots of people believe. These people have passed through our elementary and secondary school systems since the 1960s and are thoroughly indoctrinated to believe we are using too much of the sun's energy.

They believe, as does Ms. Sawin, "There is only so much energy on Earth, and all the interconnected, complicated, essential parts of the living system cannot survive without a share of it." Do you think we are running out of the Sun's energy? Do you think there's only just so much energy to be had that we have to completely alter all human activity to insure there's enough for the geese and the dolphins?

Let me tell you a little bit about the Sun. It is a ball of hot gases and is 865,000 miles in diameter. It makes up more than 99.9 percent of the mass in our solar system—this is necessary to insure that its gravitational attraction is great enough to hold the entire system together. It is a star of "average" temperature, about 15,000,000 degrees Celsius in its interior and about 6000 degrees Celsius at the surface. Its energy, radiating through space, is the only significant source of heat and light for the solar system. Here's where it gets worrisome. Scientists estimate that there's only some five *billion* years of energy left.

Oddly, despite its enormous generation of heat, there are whole parts of the Earth covered in ice. These places are very cold and home to polar bears and penguins. No sensible person wants to live in these places because nothing grows there. Once ice covered a much larger portion of the Earth and, until it melted sufficiently—thanks to the sun—human beings didn't even exist. Their ancestors reputedly lived in trees or ran around on all fours eating Lord knows what.

19

Alan Caruba

I tell you this because it well may be that, having passed through our educational system, you too haven't a clue about the sun, the earth, and all that dwells thereon.

Back to Ms. Sawin. The reason she "knows" that humans are using up too much of the sun's energy is that "humans co-opt 32 percent of the total solar energy captured by land plants, according to a study in the Dec. 21 issue of *Science*. Ecologists know this because they can measure the plant biomass created each year, something called the Net Primary Production, or the NPP, and estimate how much of it is diverted away from the rest of life by human activities."

Follow me closely now because you will learn why virtually everything any environmentalist or ecologist tells you is the biggest pack of lies you have heard since your husband told you you're not getting fat or your wife told you she doesn't care you're going bald.

First of all, the article she cites appeared in *Science*, a magazine that, like *Scientific American*, has been seriously infected by the environmental agenda to the point that much of what it offers as proof of anything requires heavy duty, critical examination and deconstruction. The notion that the Net Primary Production index or whatever they call it can accurately measure plant biomass is ludicrous. Can you imagine anyone being able to determine with certainty the use of solar energy by all the grasses, plants and forests of the earth? No, of course, you can't.

This is a typical environmental propaganda device, much like the computer models cited to prove global warming is happening. It sounds scientific. It looks scientific. It is a load of crap.

However, the Elizabeth Sawin's of the world will continue to worry that "the solar energy flowing through a cornfield won't find its way to some of the specialized birds and insects that populate a prairie, because those prairie creatures don't have the faintest idea what to do with corn stalks or corn earworms."

If this strikes you as idiotic, go to the front of the class, put a gold star beside your name, and return to your seat satisfied in the knowledge that you are not as big an idiot as Ms. Sawin. Then go home and bake some cornbread muffins. Hmmmmm, good!

Too Many Precautions Will Kill You

With the relentless passion of true believers, self-appointed environmental and health activists are busy promoting a potent new weapon in their ongoing war against business, technology, and progress. Known euphemistically as the "Precautionary Principle," it is the latest manifestation of how these radicals obscure their real intentions by swathing them in the rhetoric of risk, fear, environmental destruction, and utopian dreams of safety through ever-expanding regulation.

Begin first by understanding that it is not a "principle" at all. It is the invention of radical Greens and others who conjure up these devices in order to impose their agendas upon the unwitting who actually believe their lies.

The Precautionary Principle totally abandons the time-tested scientific method that separates fact from fiction. Rather than placing faith in science, it employs the rhetoric of fear to wreak havoc on the lives of ordinary people. Its true purpose is to thwart invention and innovation, keeping new and improved products and services off the market.

In practice, it will further control consumer and lifestyle choices. Ultimately, it will put people's lives at risk.

In the hands of activist pressure groups, bureaucrats, lawyers and judges, the Precautionary Principle focuses solely on the POSSIBILITY that a risk MIGHT exist. Mere allegations of a threat, however small or theoretical, will automatically trigger endless delays or outright bans. If enacted as law, our freedom and our right to ask "How much risk?" "Is the risk real?" and "Are the benefits greater than the risks?" would cease to exist.

The Precautionary Principle is the exact *opposite* of science which requires evidence, clear links and probable cause, and then measures levels of actual or potential risk. It holds that all products and activities are dangerous until proven absolutely safe, guilty until proven innocent.

True progress has *always* been about taking risks in order to reduce or eliminate greater risks. Had the Precautionary Principle been in force during the past century, we'd have no electrical power, no x-rays or

CAT-scans, no polio or measles vaccines, open heart surgery or organ transplants, and certainly no pesticides, cars or airplanes!

The environmentalists and so-called consumer advocates say they'd never interpret the "principle" that way, but their actions speak louder than their protestations. For example, in the late 1980s, Green activists convinced Peruvian authorities to stop chlorinating their nation's drinking water, claiming that chlorine posed a "potential" cancer risk. The result was a cholera epidemic that infected over a million people and killed thousands.

In 1972, Greens succeeded in banning DDT. Previously, it had all but eliminated malaria in many Asian and African countries. Malaria returned with a vengeance. According to the World Health Organization, during the past three decades at least 30 million people have died from malaria in Third World nations, especially Africa. Half were children under the age of five. A simple, cheap, effective application of DDT would have saved their lives.

Donald Roberts, professor of public health at the Uniformed Services University in Bethesda, Maryland, says, "Not using DDT is criminal." For the Greens, however, preventing millions of deaths takes a back seat to their rabid anti-pesticide, anti-progress ideology.

From the "Alar" hoax about apples, to claims that cell phones cause brain damage, to attacks on genetically modified foods and seeds, to allegations about phthalates in plastics, the Greens continue to seek every way possible to thwart any progress that might benefit mankind. In the process, they perpetrate a form of benign genocide.

There is one final reason why Americans (and others around the world) should resist every effort to impose the Precautionary Principle. Science-based caution has always been the foundation of U.S. regulatory policy, insuring that a careful weighing of real evidence for potential harm and benefits will govern our consumer, health, environmental, and agricultural rules.

The Precautionary Principle would destroy a system that has blessed Americans with the best health and longest life expectancy in world history. Its enactment as the basic for regulatory law should send chills down everyone's spine.

The United Nations

THE UN 'MILLENNIUM SUMMIT' THREATENS U.S. NATIONAL SOVEREIGNTY

O n June 21, 1788, the United States Constitution became effective after New Hampshire became the ninth State to ratify it. It is the oldest functioning constitution in existence and it has afforded every citizen guarantees of freedom virtually unknown in most of the world today.

On September 6th - 8th, 2000, the heads of state of many nations from around the world gathered at the United Nations "Millennium Summit" in New York to "sign, ratify or accede" to the multilateral conventions deposited with the Secretary General of the United Nations.

By 2000, there were *514 multilateral treaties* involved, the majority of which have been adopted by the UN General Assembly. A "core group" of these consists of twenty-five treaties and their purpose is nothing less than to change the existing UN Charter for the purpose of creating a global government to end the rights of sovereignty and self-government of all nations. The rationale and rhetoric supporting this are the lies of communism. Were the United States to agree to the aims of the "Millennium Summit", your rights as a U.S. citizen would cease to exist.

What most Americans do not know is that all but one of the seventeen

23

U.S. Department of State diplomats who helped shaped the original UN were later identified as *secret members of the Communist Party, USA*. The UN's first Secretary General, Alger Hiss, was *a Soviet agent*. In its 54-year history, all seven Secretary Generals of the UN have been either dedicated socialists or communists. All 15 of the UN Under-Secretary-Generals for Political and Security Council Affairs, in charge of UN military affairs, have been communists and all but one has come from either the former Soviet Union or the current Russian Federation. Fully two-thirds of the membership of the General Assembly, the Security Council, and the World Court have always been representatives of socialist and communist nations.

What chance do democracy and capitalism have under such circumstances? None!

By 1999, not one single American held a top decision-making post at the United Nations over peacekeeping, economic or social programs. The U.S. pays an estimated one quarter to one third of *all* UN costs. Just in terms of peacekeeping activities, the UN owes American taxpayers almost $15 billion. This amount is equal to the UN pension fund for its employees, among whom is the former Nazi and Secretary General, Kurt Waldheim, who continues to draw a $102,000 UN pension.

The 'Millennium Summit' is the culmination of years of effort to install a global government upon the world that would fulfill the objectives of communism; a failed economic system and one kept in place by authoritarianism. The world would be ruled by a UN with all power ceded to a "People's Assembly" composed of representatives of non-governmental-organizations (NGOs).

In April 2000, *The Earth Times*, subsidized by *The New York Times*, carried a front page article titled "Outsiders on the Inside", identifying the organizations that determine UN policy and programs. They represent some of the biggest foundations in the United States including those such as the David and Lucile Packard Foundation, the William H. Gates Foundation, the Ford Foundation, the John D. and Catherine T. MacArthur Foundation, the Howard Heinz Endowments, the Pew Charitable Trusts, and the Rockefeller Foundation. These and other foundations, all based on the enormous economic engine of capitalism are funding a socialist and communist organ bent on global government.

The list of NGOs who would ultimately rule is so vast you need to visit the web site of Sovereignty International to examine it. It includes radical environmental organizations, groups devoted to controlling the world's population, and countless others who pursue agendas so foreign to American values they would destroy everything for which Americans have fought and died to preserve and protect.

At its core, the UN is anti-American. Its main body, the Security Council, is manipulated by Russia and China who use their veto power to the detriment of American interests. The other main body, the General Assembly, is comprised of 188 nations, some of whom have populations less than the States of New Jersey or Rhode Island. The third element of power at the UN is the Secretary-General. Kofi Annan has functioned as a foreign agent for Iraq, permitting it to remain a member in good standing despite its flaunting of UN restrictions on its efforts to produce weapons of mass destruction, and turning a blind eye to the primary sponsor of terrorism, Iran.

The 'Millennium Summit' would drastically alter even this sinister power structure. It would strip the Security Council of its veto power and, in doing so, remove the last instrument of control the U.S. would have, along with its status as a permanent member.

The 'Millennium Summit' would grant the UN oversight, i.e. control, of all of the earth's land, air and seas. They will vote to give the UN oversight of international conflicts despite its long record of dismal failures. The Summit will grant the UN power over all financial institutions, commerce, trade relations, labor relations, education and private property. The U.S. Congress, the States, and all communities throughout America would exist solely to carry out the mandates of the UN.

By now, you may be asking yourself why you have read practically *nothing* in the mainstream press of this nation? Why, with the future of national and worldwide sovereignty at stake, has the "Millennium Summit" been ignored? Why have we heard nothing from the White House or the members of Congress who should be speaking out against this attack on the U.S. Constitution?

One reason might be because *56 members of Congress are dedicated socialists*, members of the Democratic Socialists of America! (www.dusa.org). It is the largest socialist organization in the nation and the principle U.S. affiliate of the Socialist International. As for the President and Vice President, their actions have demonstrated their leftist commitment to the goals of a New World Order.

What Lenin and Stalin could not impose on the world, what Hitler could not impose on the world, will be enacted at the United Nations "Millennium Summit" on September 6th through the 8th. The only way to avoid this is for the United States Congress to vote to withdraw from the United Nations. When that occurs, the entire house of cards will fall. The UN cannot exist financially without the support it receives from us taxpayers. The UN is the enemy of the United States and freedom-living people everywhere in the world. This sham, perpetrated on the world by communists and their sympathizers, must end.

The new millennium that has dawned must be dedicated to freedom. But first we must free ourselves from the threat of global government by un-elected individuals and groups who would enslave us all.

The UN: Irrelevant & Malignant

The United States with a population in excess of 287 million people has one vote in the United Nations General Assembly. There are 188 other members. Of these, 130 member nations have populations less than 13 million people. That is less than the State of Florida. Their vote is equal to that of the USA.

It gets worse; there are 31 nations with a full vote that have less than a half million people (500,000). Even our least populated State, Wyoming, has more people. These UN member nations have the same vote as the U.S., China, India, Russia, Great Britain Japan or any other major power in the world. Indeed, fourteen nations with less than 100,000 people have a vote equal to ours. They include Tuvalu (10,836), San Marino (26,937) and Liechtenstein (31,130).

The real power is in the UN Security Council, composed of permanent members, Great Britain, France, China, Russia, and the United States. All of them, except the U.S., are Socialist/Communist nations. There are ten other members elected for two-year terms. The one question no one has been able to answer for me is "How much security has the UN provided the world since its inception in 1947?"

The UN Charter says it exists to "save succeeding generations from the scourge of war…to practice tolerance and live together in peace as good neighbors, to unite our strength to maintain international peace and security." This malignancy that passes for an international organization devoted to fostering peace and a bunch of other noble ideals has proven to be utterly useless and totally irrelevant, except as a threat to democracy and freedom everywhere.

These days, the UN is totally devoted to transforming itself into a global government, essentially ending the sovereignty of all member and non-member nations through a matrix of treaties, conferences, and protocols. The UN has its hand in all aspects of life on Earth from trade to the environment. It wants the right to tax everyone, to have its own judicial system, and its own military capability. If it has its way, you will be saluting the UN flag, not the Stars and Stripes.

Founded after World War II, its architects were either Soviets or secret agents of the Soviets, working at the highest levels within the U.S. State Department. Its first, interim Secretary General was none other than Alger Hiss who went to jail for lying about the fact that he was a Soviet agent. The United Nations has never had a Secretary General who wasn't a dedicated Socialist.

The first major conflict that broke out after WWII was the invasion by communist North Korea of South Korea. U.S. troops are still stationed there more than a half-century later after the "United Nations Police Action" that threw the North Koreans and the Red Chinese army back behind the 38th parallel. Frankly, there isn't room to recount all the other so-called United Nations' efforts to maintain the peace that weren't totally dependent on the strength of the United States to achieve any resolution.

The five wars waged against Israel alone are a testimony to the UN's ability to look the other way when a member nation is fighting for its life. There is no single organization in the world that is more anti-Semitic than the United Nations. Its conference "against" racism, held in Durban, South Africa, last year was such a horror of racism, mostly aimed at Israel, the U.S. withdrew its representatives. Between 1967 and 1988, there were 88 Security Council resolutions passed against Israel and not one criticizing a single Arab nation or the PLO. In that same time span, the General Assembly passed 429 anti-Israel resolutions.

In the years since the UN was founded, there have been appalling genocides in Asia and Africa. When the United States was attacked by al Qaeda, the U.S. did not go to the General Assembly to ask permission to respond; it sent its military to Afghanistan to decimate this threat. The U.S. had learned the lesson of the Gulf War during which, operating under a UN resolution, it was not permitted to go into Baghdad and kill Saddam Hussein and his gang of thugs. Told by Iraq to leave, following its failed invasion of Kuwait, the UN withdrew its inspection teams searching for weapons of mass destruction.

No one seems too upset by this, except of course, those of us who keep calling for the complete withdrawal by the U.S. from the UN. This perfectly sane response to what is clearly an evil organization invariably earns us the knee-jerk nomenclature of "extreme right wingers."

What is "extreme" about opposing an institution that has not only utterly failed to bring about peace, has made no impact on the abuse of human rights around the world, and which poses a threat to our republic? The United Nations is an international malignancy, undermining free societies everywhere, a platform for racism, a mechanism seeking transfer the wealth of industrialized nations to those that do not foster any economic growth of their own.

Remember that the next time the U.S. Ambassador to the United Nations casts our one vote in the General Assembly at the same time as Djibouti.

Are You Ready to Pay Your UN Taxes?

When I took the oath of duty for my service in the United States Army, I swore to uphold and protect the U.S. Constitution. It was made clear to me that I was not to serve any foreign kings or potentates. My sole allegiance was to the United States of America.

One of these days, if the United Nations' potentates have their way, I am going to receive a tax bill that will include a portion of my earnings allocated to the UN. Their taxation powers will have been imposed as a new layer on top of those paid to the United States.

As it is, my tax dollars and yours already contribute to the dues paid by the U.S.; a full 22 percent of the entire bill to maintain the UN, but not including the money we give to UNESCO, nor the millions to fund the many military missions we undertake for the UN, but for which we rarely, if ever, receive compensation.

In 2001, the U.S. was voted off the UN Human Rights Commission, a seat it held from its beginning in 1948. It has lost its seat on the UN International Narcotics Board and now comes word that it may lose its leadership role with the UN World Food Program where we contributed $24 million last year, more than any other nation. The General Accounting Office is about to release a report that former President Clinton diverted

$24 billion, meant for our military, for UN peacekeeping missions around the world from 1995 to 2001. The "official" amount we are said to have contributed is $3.45 billion.

The notion that this nation owes any dues to the UN is a fraud. Had I any choice, not one cent of my money would go to the upkeep of the UN.

For Americans and others around the world, if the UN's High Level Panel of Financing Development has its way, this global octopus will spread its tentacles of power to impose global taxes.

On the surface, the Panel's conference will be passed off as being about boosting foreign aid to needy Third World nations. They are needy because they are mostly run by despots who siphon off aid into their Swiss bank accounts or spend it on military hardware instead of roads and bridges, hospitals and schools.

They are needy because they oppress their own people and destroy their ability to create any kind of a middle class who might unite to demand freedom. In socialist regimes, they are provided with enough "free" services to keep them (in theory) content.

The treaties and protocols created by this "Development" conference will be added to the more than 175 that already directly affect the internal policies of the United States of America, its individual States, and your local government.

(1) They intend to create an International Tax Organization. My Father was a Certified Public Accountant. Every year, until he retired, he wrestled with an increasingly complex tax code issued by the Internal Revenue Service. I learned to keep receipts for everything from him. Can you imagine trying to deal with a United Nations tax code?

(2) They intend to levy global taxes and they have their eyes on those that would affect every single financial transaction (currency) and on all energy use. These taxes would most affect industrialized nations by redistributing the funds to those for whom capitalism is an anathema. It isn't taxation. It's theft.

(3) They are calling for something they call "tax harmonization." This would permit high-tax nations, Socialists, to require their system be imposed on all income earned in the United States. Thus, the welfare states of Europe and the corrupt Third World nations would bring all their economic woes to bear on the citizens of the

U.S.. Right now, the President is calling for lower taxes in order to stimulate our economy. Under the rules being proposed by the United Nations, this nation would not have their power.

(4) If someone from another nation moved to the United States, the UN conference will propose that their earnings be taxed to ensure the payment would be made to the nation they fled!

The conference will also call for the United States to increase its foreign aid to "the annual equivalent of 0.7 percent of industrialized countries' gross national product." This means our current level of foreign aid would rise from $12 billion annually to more than $70 billion!

None of the language of the proposals that will be put forth at the UN conference make any reference at all to lowering tax rates, a vital element for economic development, nor will it discuss controlling wasteful government spending.

This conference is about DESTROYING the economic strength of the United States and the restructuring of our economic system to resemble the welfare states of England, France, Germany and nations whose governments take up to 70 percent ore more of the earnings of their citizens. They then redistribute it into programs such as socialized medicine that simply do not work.

The conference is about controlling all multinational corporations, all international transactions, turning them into cash cows for the United Nations.

The United States has exactly one vote in the UN General Assembly. The vast number of the other 185 nations would be the primary beneficiaries of this scheme to deprive Americans of the right to determine what their tax codes will be and how their tax dollars are spent.

Most Americans have no idea they are barely a month away from this act of global government grand theft.

A treaty begins life officially when the UN General Assembly or a special conference adopts the final draft of a proposed treaty. This draft is then circulated to member nations for their "signatures." Delegates from the participating nations "sign" the document, thus indicating their nation's intent to "ratify" it. The signature does not bind the nation to the terms of the treaty, but it does obligate the nation to "take *no action contrary* to the treaty."

Americans are being duped into accepting restrictions that can do nothing more than increase the cost of the use of all forms of energy by this nation. If there isn't a massive outcry against the forthcoming UN "Development" conference, we will all end up paying taxes to the United Nations.

There is only one solution. The United States must withdraw from the United Nations or it will be subsumed into its plan to determine every aspect of life here and in every other nation of the world. We will end up paying for our own enslavement. There can be no halfway steps toward accommodation. Wendell Phillips said, "Eternal vigilance is the price of liberty." We are about to lose ours.

Indicting the United Nations

The hypocrisy and torrent of lies coming out of the United Nations conference on racism should, one think, wake up Americans and others in Western nations to the reality of this insidious institution. Unfortunately, in the affairs of men, it doesn't work that way. Only those with a passion for liberty and justice pay notice to its enemies.

It is long past the time when the United Nations should have been allowed die of its own inertia and evil intentions. Much has been made of the racism conference's use as a podium for that most ancient of hatreds, the slanders heaped upon Jews. Fostered by a dozen Middle Eastern nations, this calumny has managed to drive other issues into the background, but there never was any need for the conference. Racism exists everywhere and not one thousand conferences will eradicate it. This UN conference is simply an excuse to advance anti-Semitism, the grievances of black peoples against whites, and comparable complaints.

Largely unnoticed is the xenophobia that exists on a daily basis at the United Nations. While the UN constantly hectors the U.S. to send money that constitutes 25 percent of its budget, Americans hold only 7.2 percent of its more than 56,000 jobs. A study by the General Accounting Office determined that at the senior, decision-making level only 2,076 Americans, 9.5 percent, hold such positions. This prejudice exists throughout the UN's operations. The World Food Program, for which the U.S. provides more than half of its funding, is staffed by 90 percent of non-American personnel who, every year, find it difficult to account for tons of food that simply goes

31

missing.

Earlier this year (2001), the United States' seat on the UN Human Rights Commission was lost. The U.S. had held a seat since its inception in 1947. A number of African nations where human rights are non-existent nonetheless hold seats on this commission, along with Cuba and that great paragon of human rights, the Peoples Republic of China. Rejection of the U.S. should have signaled Congress that it was time to leave, but it the only action it took was to vote to withhold $242 million in UN dues until the U.S. seat is restored.

Meanwhile, the UN continues its effort to ban several private human rights advocacy groups from participating as non-governmental organizations. Among them are Freedom House, the Baptist World Alliance, the Simon Weisenthal Center and the Family Research Council. The effort is being led by a 19-nation subcommittee of the UN Economic and Social Council.

In August, a spokesman for the UN Population Fund, Sven Burnester, told British reporters that "For all the bad press, China has achieved the impossible. The country has solved its population problem." This is consistent with the view that the world's real problem is the human race. Meanwhile, the forced abortions, sterilization, and the outright killing of new-borns, continues as a state-endorsed one-child-only program throughout Red China, though to the credit of ordinary Chinese, it is still widely flouted.

The drive toward a global "environmental governance" program continues. In the same way the UN conjured up the Kyoto Treaty on Climate Control, an insidious instrument intended to force Western, industrialized nations to destroy their economies, the UN Environmental Program (UNEP) has convened an "expert consultants" procedure that always precedes the creation of yet another noxious treaty. This one would be introduced at the June 2002 World Summit on Sustainable Development. The goal of this treaty would be to turn the UNEP into the UN equivalent of the World Trade Organization, but one which would give environmental groups the opportunity to impose restrains on trade in favor of environment mandates.

Americans remain blithely unaware of a vast matrix of United Nations treaties, some of which actually cede our national sovereignty in ways that would astound and appall them. For example, in 1972, the U.S. signed the UN World Heritage Treaty. It created "World Heritage Sites" and "Biosphere Reserves." Selected for their cultural, historical or natural significance, national governments are obligated to protect these landmarks. Since 1972, 68 percent of all U.S. national parks, monuments and preserves have been designated World Heritage Sites.

Among those that fall under the ultimate control of the United Nations are the Statue of Liberty, Thomas Jefferson's home at Monticello, the Washington Monument, the Brooklyn Bridge, Yellowstone National Park, the Florida Everglades, and the Grand Canyon.

When the Crown Buttes Mines wanted to mine for gold in Montana, that project to access this nation's valuable natural resource was thwarted by the United Nations at the request of the Clinton Administration. The mine, it said, was too close to Yellowstone. The project would have employed 280 people and generated $230 million in revenue. This was a direct attack on the company's property rights under the U.S. Constitution and ignored a U.S. federal law prohibiting the inclusion of non-federal property within a U.S. World Heritage Site without the consent of the property owner.

The United Nations has made no secret of its intent to be the sole government of the entire world. The report of the UN Commission on Global Governance, *Our Global Neighborhood*, was published by the Oxford University Press in 1995. There you will find plans for the UN World Court endorsed by the Clinton Administration, an independent military free to invade any nation that will not cede its freedom to the UN, and, of course, a system of worldwide taxation to fund this monstrosity.

The litany of the United Nations hypocrisy and its patient, creeping effort to control the world could fill several books.

The real question is when, if ever, Americans will wake to the danger it represents and demand U.S. withdrawal from this vile international institution? Few know that it is the creation of the then Soviet Union in cooperation with known U.S. Soviet agents in our State Department. If you think Communism is dead, just visit the UN headquarters in New York. It is there that the end of any real hope of liberty for the peoples of the world is being plotted

Alan Caruba

A History of Hostility:
The United Nations vs. Israel

In December 2001, many United Nations ambassadors in New York, Geneva, and Vienna marked the "International Day of Solidarity with the Palestinian People" and called for the establishment of a Palestinian State.

On May 14, 1948, the United Nations had passed a partition plan calling for a Jewish national state in Palestine, the name designating the former protectorate administered by the British. The following day, Arab states attacked Israel. It was to be the first of several wars to destroy Israel. It also marked the beginning of the long history of hostility to Israel that reveals the UN for the sham it always was and remains today. On December 11, 1948, UN Resolution 194 was to serve as the basis for the return of Palestinians who had fled the new nation. All member Arab states voted against it.

Among the recent and most blatant examples of the UN's hostility to Israel was the UN World Conference Against Racism held during the summer of 2001 in Durban, South Africa. South Africa is a basketcase of murder and rape, and its economy has lost 90 percent of its value, after seven years of ANC rule. The conference, before it even began, was rife with anti-Semitism and anti-Israel propaganda. The United States withdrew its representatives.

In November 2001, the Associated Press reported, "Shunned by President Bush and under attack for not doing enough to combat terrorism, Palestinian leader Yasser Arafat found a receptive audience at the United Nations yesterday and the ear of the secretary-general." The current state of war against Israel by the Palestinians had already been ongoing for over a year.

Those like myself who argue that the United Nations is a threat to the national sovereignty of our own and all other nations of the world draw lessons from the UN's constant rejection of Israel. Its General Assembly and many commissions have shown unstinting hostility to this member nation, never ceding even its right to exist. Its self-defense is always identified as an attack on Palestinians, a group of Arabs within Israel who, if they wished, could enjoy full citizenship in the only democracy in the Middle East. There are Arab members of the Knesset, the governing body of Israel.

Historically, however, the General Assembly has served as a forum to isolate and rebuke Israel. In November 1975, a UN resolution equated Zionism (the political movement to establish and maintain Israel as a home for Jews) as a form of racism and racial discrimination. For the record, Judaism is a religion, not a race. It would take until 1991 to repeal this calumny.

In the early 1990's, as so-called progress toward peace with its neighbors began, the UN's hostility began to wane somewhat as the Madrid and Oslo processes, along with the end of the Cold War, began to take shape. The powerful Soviet-Arab coalition had collapsed along with the then-Soviet Union. Both Israelis and Palestinians signed an historical Declaration of Principles in 1993 and the condemnations of Israel abated and anti-Semitism was declared a form of racism by the UN's Human Rights Commission.

For the first time since it was founded in 1948, Israel was able to participate in UN affairs by being named to its first UN committee in 1993. On December 14, 1993, 155 member nations endorsed the Israel-Palestinian and Israel-Jordan agreements. Earlier it had amended a large group of anti-Israel resolutions that had come to be known as the "Question of Palestine."

As the violence perpetrated by Palestinians began to rise, the passed year and a half has seen renewed efforts in the UN to condemn the Israelis. Opposition to the U.S. decision to move its embassy to Jerusalem was expressed. A resolution concerning Jerusalem, the nation's capital, said "The decision of Israel to impose its laws, jurisdiction and administration on the Holy City of Jerusalem is illegal ... and null and void." Jerusalem's status goes back some 3,500 years as the ancient capital and, for those who read their Bible, is frequently cited as such.

Demands that Israel withdraw from territories occupied as the result of the war in 1967 perpetrated against it by Arab states have never ended. The General Assembly voted in 1996 emphasizing the "inalienable rights" of the Palestinians. The Israeli UN ambassador summed up the situation saying, "the United Nations is a convenient and willing forum for bypassing the peace process."

As we now know, there never truly was, nor is there now, any peace process so far as the Palestinians are concerned. Their existence is predicated on the destruction of Israel. On April 20, 2001, the UN condemned the "disproportionate and indiscriminate" use of force by Israel in the so-called occupied territories. No mention is ever made of the terror bombings and other acts of aggression against Israel.

On February 21st of this year, Kofi Annan was again calling for a "just, lasting and comprehensive peaceful settlement," but just ten days earlier, the UN Committee on the Exercise of Inalienable Rights of the Palestinian People declared through its chairman, that "the committee was more determined than ever to fulfill its mandate to give back to the Palestinian people all of their inalienable rights." Presumably, this means giving them the entire landmass of the nation of Israel.

All this suggests that the United Nations is one of the most biased and useless international institutions on the face of the earth today. Nothing about it addresses its supposed mission to secure world peace. Everything about it is moving inexorably toward establishing itself as a world government. When that happens, you can kiss the U.S. Constitution goodbye. Or, if you live elsewhere in the world, whatever freedoms you assume your government will provide and protect.

Energy Issues

Windmills of the Mindless

A brief blackout of electricity due to a storm in my area left me in a house in which the lights didn't work, nor the computer, nor anything else. Without electricity, I was thrust back to a time when burning wood in the fireplace was the only source of warmth and only way to cook a meal. Think about that the next time some idiot talks about alternative forms of energy.

The cabal of environmental organizations in collusion with the Democrats has succeeded in denying Americans the ability to tap billions of barrels of its own oil. It has already managed to drive out many mining operations in the nation. The environment will be the primary issue Democrats will pursue in the November elections and they will be lying to you.

To listen to the environmentalists—Greens—talk you would think that there weren't billions of barrels of oil reserves yet untapped around the world. You would think it was a good idea to be reliant on the tender mercies of Saudi Arabia, Iraq, Iran and other nations who, last time I checked, hated the U.S. You would think that the U.S. doesn't have centuries' worth of coal as yet untapped.

Brace yourself to listen to environmentalists talk endlessly about the need for all of us to drive around in very small cars that use very little gasoline or, worse, to waste more millions on ethanol, made from corn, grown and processed with prodigious amounts of energy, in order to "save" energy. The leader of the pack, Al Gore, wants to "eliminate the internal combustion engine." The enemy that the Greens are most determined to eliminate are cars, trucks and vans.

You will hear much talk of solar energy and the use of the wind power. These are the so-called "alternative" sources of energy. Before you fall for this Green scam, you better read Dr. Howard C. Hayden's book, *The Solar Fraud: Why Solar Energy Won't Run the World* ($21.95, Vales Lake Publishing LLC, PO Box 7595, Pueblo West, CO 81007-0595). Dr. Hayden is a Professor Emeritus of Physics from the University of Connecticut and Adjunct Professor at the University of Southern Colorado. He publishes a monthly newsletter, *The Energy Advocate*, now in its sixth year. What he doesn't know about energy and its production isn't worth knowing.

"The solar fraud is the litany of unrealistic, rosy predictions of a solar future. It involves lying with statistics and attempting to manipulate the public through numerous coercive means. It is a sure path to Brownout Nirvana."

The U.S. has an enormous capacity for producing the energy we require for everything. Fully 40 percent of our electricity is produced by burning coal. The Clinton Administration put vast deposits of high grade coal off limits to use in Utah. We also have vast hydroelectric capabilities and, if we had any sense at all, we would be building nuclear generators that don't "pollute" at all.

"Together, photovoltaics, wind power, wood burning and waste burning in 1998 resulted in a mere 1.6 percent of the electricity used in the U.S.," writes Dr. Hayden. "For industries, homes, commercial establishments, and utilities, the total 1998 contribution from wind and direct solar energy (of all kinds) was one part in every 862—0.116 percent—of the total U.S. energy budget."

With refreshing candor, Dr. Hayden notes that "If the world's citizens were suddenly to stop using coal, oil, natural gas, nuclear power, hydropower, geothermal power, firewood, direct solar heat, photovoltaics, animal labor, and all other sources of energy, there would be no trucks, trains, boats, or animals to deliver food or anything else."

"There would be no mechanized farming. There would be no clean water delivered to homes. There would be neither heat nor refrigeration. Very few people would be around at this time next year to comment about it. People would die off by the billions."

You can't say it any more plainly, but be assured that you and everyone else are going to continue to be assailed with the lies of the Greens who will insist we don't need that oil in Alaska. These enemies of our nation will tell you that, not only do we need to continue paying billions to Arab and Persian nations that hate us, but we need to conserve, conserve, conserve. You cannot conserve your way to anything but darkness when it comes to energy use.

Before you start thinking windmills are the wave of the future, Dr. Hayden reminds you that "California has some huge windmills—some 3200 of them—covering mountain sides in their windy areas. All together, they produce—at a rare full wind—about 300 MW, which is about 1/4 as much power as a moderately large nuclear power plant produces, and is less than 10 percent of the electricity the small state of Connecticut consumes."

Ask the Greens and they will tell you we mustn't build any nuclear energy producing utilities and, of course, hydroelectric utilities threaten fish and require dams. They are opposed to coal and all mining activity. If we listen to these traitors and idiots all of our remarkable, life-enhancing technologies will have to be abandoned. This is nothing less than a policy for national energy suicide. It is a policy that Congress has just endorsed with its vote against drilling in a tiny part of Alaska

"The most dangerous aspect of energy is not using it," says Dr. Hayden. He's right.

The World has More Oil, Not Less

The truth about oil is that the world has more, not less, waiting to be discovered, extracted, and used to the benefit of mankind.

Why, then, are we being told that we have to cut back consumption? The answer is political, not geological. Even a casual look at the UN Kyoto Climate Control Treaty reveals the economic devastation that would occur if this nation and other industrialized nations were forced to cut back to 1990 levels of energy use. Under the Kyoto UN Treaty, economists warn that gasoline prices would rise far higher than they are today. Electricity costs would increase anywhere between 20 percent and 86 percent. The cost of natural gas would rise between 20 percent and 148 percent.

The leading advocate for the UN Climate Control Treaty is Vice President Al Gore. Even if one were to ignore the questions regarding his truthfulness, his environmental dementia, if he were elected, would initiate a worldwide economic Depression.

Globally, we need *more* energy, not less. The good news is, if you factor in coal as the primary source of the generation of electricity, you're actually looking at not just hundreds, but thousands of years of electrical power. Coal is so abundant it is measured in the thousands of years of use. Abundant electrical power will free Third World nations from their poverty. It will benefit the lives of millions who are denuding the forests of their nations for fuel to cook dinner!

There is no truth to the reports that the Earth is running out of oil.

In 1973, an oil field was discovered off the coast of Louisiana in a deep area of the Gulf of Mexico. By 1989, oil production had trickled down to a daily output of only 4,000 barrels. Then, to the surprise and delight of the PennzEnergy Company, the Eugene Island Field began to pump 13,000 barrels a day. Geologists tested the new crude and discovered it was a completely different geological age than the original oil of ten years earlier!

Now petroleum scientists are beginning to believe there is a whole new oil supply streaming from a vast source many miles below the surface of the Earth. The ramifications of this are obvious. There is a lot of oil as yet undiscovered and untapped.

This phenomenon explains why Middle East oil reserves doubled since the 1980's, currently estimated to be about two thirds of a trillion barrels. A Cornell University professor emeritus, Thomas Gold, believes that oil is manufactured deep in the earth under extreme pressure and heat. As it interacts with bacteria, it oozes up to the surface, appearing to be prehistoric, but actually "new" in geological terms.

The latest figures set the "proven crude oil reserves" of the Middle East at about 686.4 thousand million barrels. Saudi Arabia sits on top of 261.5 thousand million. Kuwait has 112.5 thousand million. The estimates of the untapped crude in Alaska are set at about 16 billion barrels. The area involved is one tenth of one percent of the entire area of the State. Are you really so worried about some caribou, grizzly bears, and rabbits that you aren't willing to tap into a tiny part of that huge reserve?

On a Royal Dutch/Shell Group floating platform a hundred miles off the coast of Louisiana where oil production wasn't even feasible a few years ago, there are estimates of 100 billion barrels of untapped crude oil. At this point, 40 billion barrels have already been discovered in deep waters worldwide from West Africa to Brazil to the Gulf of Mexico. In the Gulf of Mexico alone, production could rise at as much as 1.8 million barrels a day by 2001. This is double the 1995 level and roughly equal to the daily output of Kuwait.

So, do you still think we're running out of oil? The simple arithmetic of oil production is that we keep finding more and more of it.

My friend, Robert L. Bradley, Jr., the director of the Institute for Energy Research, recently authored *Julian Simon and the Triumph of Energy Sustainability*. It puts the skids to all the crisis talk and lies environmentalists have spread about "sustainability." That is a Green code word for shutting down any progress toward providing even more abundant (and needed) energy for a world that is being brought together by the Internet and other means of communication and transportation.

"All environmental indicators concerning the use of hydrocarbons— whether they involve land use, spillage, wastage or combustion—are demonstrating positive trends and in many cases exceeding expectations," says Bradley. "Consumers are embracing multiple new uses of energy in transportation and stationary markets. Risk management opportunities and mass customization of energy products are multiplying. Safety and productivity are improving throughout these industries. All these trends appear to be open-ended."

That's how the prospects for more oil stand now, open-ended. Since the manufactured crisis of the 1970's, we have found billions more barrels of oil. More is yet to be found in this decade and beyond, waiting to ooze up to the surface where it can be accessed for future generations.

Right now, our own and other governments around the world that do not invest in its discovery, its extraction, its transportation, its refining or in its sale, other than to impose taxes on every stage are extorting more money than even the profits made by oil companies. If, however, the marketplace was allowed to determine a fair price, there will be sufficient oil, sufficient natural gas, and more than sufficient coal to power a period of unparalleled worldwide prosperity. It would also cost the consumer far less.

The Price of Water vs. the Price of Oil

There are lots of mistaken ideas about oil and we need to dispel a few of them, starting with the myth that the Earth is running out of oil.

In fact, rather than being "unsustainable," the Earth may well be producing new quantities of oil as you read this. Geologists are beginning to conclude just that.

Writing in the *Houston Chronicle* in April 2002, a friend of mine, Robert L. Bradley Jr., president of the Houston-based Institute for Energy Research in Houston, noted that had "recently compared prices in gallon equivalents at a local supermarket that had gas pumps in the parking lot. Bottled water was going for between $6.90 per gallon for the store label, to about $6.30 for a gallon with something with a French-sounding name.

"The price of a gallon of milk ranged from $2.80 to $4, orange juice from $5 to $6, and a gallon of beer from $5 to more than $14. A gallon of the kind of wine you can buy by the gallon cost $9.50, while top-of-the-line champagne was going for more than $650 per gallon!"

"The price of gasoline outside range from $1.40 for regular to $1.60 for supreme. Subtracting the $0.38 federal and state tax put the price of regular down to about $1 per gallon."

Not only is oil cheaper than some bottled water, but consider what we get from a single barrel of crude oil.

Gasoline: 19.4 percent. Is used as fuel for trucks, cars, and boats.

Distillate fuel oil: 9.7 percent. is used for home heating oil, farm trackers, industrial machinery, electric utilities, railroads, ships, and construction and military equipment.

Kerosene-type jet fuel: 4.3 percent. Keeps airlines and military jets flying.

Residual fuel oil: 1.9 percent. Fuel for power plants, used by tankers and other large vessels. Also heats large apartment buildings.

Liquefied refinery gases: 1.9 percent. Propane, used in devices such as barbecue grills.

Still gas: 1.8 percent. An alternative fuel at refineries.

Asphalt and road oils: 1.4 percent. Fills those potholes, makes highways.

Petrochemical feedstocks: 1.1 percent. These are used in countless household items, including kitchen water filters and laminated countertops. They are used in the manufacture of synthetic fiber for clothes, the dyes used to color them, as well as perfumes and flavors. Think "plastics."

Lubricants: 0.5 percent. This is the grease that makes sure big equipment in factories and everywhere else runs smoothly.

Kerosene: 0.2 percent. Used in heat lanterns and light lamps.

Other: 0.4 percent. Used to manufacture paints, antifreeze, and other products.

Looked at in this fashion, the irrational hatred of petroleum that is one of the primary themes of environmentalism begins to look as crazy as it actually is.

Try contemplating living in a world deprived of the many uses of petroleum.

Try to figure out why the Democrat-controlled Congress will not allow the extraction of an estimated 16 billion barrels of oil lying below the surface of Alaska's barren, frozen tundra?

Do you know where our oil really comes from? According to a July 2002 issue of *Parade* magazine, in 2001 nearly 50 percent of the oil Americans use came from Canada, Mexico and Venezuela. Another 18 percent came from Angola, Britain, Nigeria, and Norway. Our number one single source of oil, however, is Saudi Arabia at 18 percent, while 8 percent came from Iraq.

We need to shift this reliance on Saudi Arabian oil to Russian oil, the second largest exporter of oil. Then we can sit back and watch the Saudis return to being camel traders.

The Old "Conserve Energy" Ploy

Just as President Bush and Vice President Cheney make the case to address the nation's too obvious energy deficit, along comes a report that we're told projects "enormous energy savings" if only the government will force us all to "conserve" in some fashion or other.

That kind of timing is just a bit too coincidental and convenient. Or haven't we learned yet how environmentalists work their magic? Whenever common sense rears its head, the Greens launch a counter-attack, armed with reports and studies by unnamed scientists.

Well, not this time, buster!

Is there anyone left in America who hasn't taken a look at California and concluded that you can't get electricity by "conserving" your way to it? California embraced every nutty conservation and alternative energy proposal that came along. And it still doesn't have enough.

Electricity happens only when you build sufficient electrical generation plants and we don't have enough right now. While we're at it, we don't need any more fuel-efficient cars. The ones we have are just fine, but we do need to make it easier for oil refineries to expand (they're currently running at 96 percent capacity) and to open areas to oil exploration and drilling.

Sunday's lead story in *The New York Times* asserted that "U.S. Scientists See Big Power Savings From Conservation." This newspaper is a contemptible reservoir of Green lies and has been for decades. There is a big price to pay for listening to and acting upon Green lies.

Writing in the Spring issue of *Citizen Outlook*, a newsletter published by the Committee for a Constructive Tomorrow, Paul Driessen examined why California is an energy basketcase. "A 1978 study for Governor Jerry Brown claimed conservation in home heating, appliances and cooling would cut California's use of natural gas and electricity by 30 percent, its peak demand by 50 percent, within 10 years. Similar pro-conservation, anti-energy development studies followed. The state believed them and acting accordingly."

So, what *really* happened? "Between 1988 and 2000, power consumption in California rose 22 percent. Demand for electrical power increased almost twice as fast as the national average." Twenty-one years after Californians fell for the "conservation" delusions of the Greens, *The New York Times* was proclaiming that, "Scientists at the country's national laboratories have projected energy savings if the government takes aggressive steps to encourage energy conservation in homes, factories, offices, appliances, cars and power plants."

Green lies die hard. In fact, they never die. The Greens are relentless in their efforts to use "government" as the means to force Americans to reduce their reliance on electrical power or to use "alternative" sources such as solar and wind power. The only problem is that these alternative sources are utter madness.

Solar and wind power are high-cost, low-efficiency energy sources. As Driessen points out "there is no way to store the electrical energy for use at night, on cloudy or windless days, and during peak usage hours; and their environmental impacts are significant." In order to produce the 218 gigawatts of *additional* electricity America will need by 2010, using only wind or solar panels, "we would have to blanket 9,400,000 acres with windmills or solar panels. That's an area equal to Connecticut, Delaware and Massachusetts combined."

The *New York Times* claims, however, that "a government-led efficiency program emphasizing research and incentives to adopt new technologies could reduce the growth in electricity demand by 20 percent to 47 percent." *Lies, just lies.* California went this route and now is in desperate need of new electrical generation plants. Its needs are currently draining the energy resources of neighboring states.

The Greens don't care how much you have to pay for electricity or gas or even food. Driving up the price is part of their game plan to force the government to step in and require that you start "conserving" even if their solutions will just end up costing you more in the long term.

You can bet the mainstream media will jump all over these new "studies" by "scientists" at "national laboratories" to convince you that this nation doesn't need to do anything except screw in a few new types of fluorescent light bulbs or start installing geothermal heat pumps or sealing buildings ever tighter. Maybe you can even read their "studies" while you are waiting in a line that's a mile long at your favorite gas station or stocking up on candles because of the latest rolling blackout.

This nation is home to mountains of coal. Enough to power a hundred new plants to provide low-cost electrical energy for centuries. We haven't even begun to seriously consider the potential of nuclear energy and we're still arguing about drilling for our own oil. Conserve? Do you really like paying more for every watt? And aren't you driving a technological wonder already? Or maybe you want to listen to the siren call of yet a new set of environmental studies?

Education Issues

Our National Education System: A $49 Billion Dollar Disaster

You had to know something was terribly wrong while you watched President George W. Bush stand at the podium and laud Sen. Teddy Kennedy. I thought he was going to stop talking just long enough to French kiss him. Nothing good can come of these two colluding on an education program and nothing will!

After you get through reading the 1000-page Education Bill, dubbed "Leave No Child Behind," you will have concluded that the Federal government is now so fully in charge of your local school system that you have only one option. You will either home school your children or you will turn them over to a system that so mirrors the Communist model for education, they will belong to Big Brother long after they have left home to create their own families.

We now have an education system in place designed to take control of children even before they enter the school system and to insure that everyone will have to conform to its dictates until they are in the grave.

Here's an interesting exercise. Sit down with a copy of the Constitution of the United States of America and see if you can find anything in it that actually authorizes the federal government to get involved in the *education* of children.

Article I, for example, spells out all kinds of things about the government, its composition of a House of Representatives and a Senate. By the time you get to section 8, it is quite specific about the powers of the Congress and no where—I repeat—no where will you find any reference to the financing of *education*.

The January 9th edition of *Education Week*, the bible of the education establishment, boasts the Bush/Kennedy education bill "sets in place requirements that will reach into virtually every public school in the nation." It goes on to note that "the mega-measure is accompanied by the largest dollar increase ever in federal education aid. The Department of Education's overall budget will rise by $6.7 billion in fiscal 2002 to nearly $49 billion." Let me repeat that: $49 *billion* dollars!

Among its mandates are grant money for programs "designed to prevent hate crimes", whatever that means. There will be money for "community-based organizations" that agree to government mandated "principles of effectiveness" if they provide pre-and-after school programs. This gobbledygook opens the door for all kinds of special interest groups to get into the education business. Those who offer tutoring services often find that public school administrators are totally indifferent to these programs, while private school administrators eagerly embrace them.

Charlotte Thomson Iserbyt is a crusader trying to alert Americans to the dangers of the education system put in place in the 1960's to totally indoctrinate every child passing through it. Here's what my friend thinks of the new education bill. It is "basically the United Nations' Lifelong Learning/Brainwashing Agenda under the umbrella of what will eventually be 'unelected' school and community councils which will make all decisions for us at the local levels." That's unelected, as in, undemocratic. Unelected as in representatives from non-government organizations that have environmental and other socialist agendas.

The end result is already on display. In Minnesota, (www.mredco.com) children have to choose their job/career track in the *8th grade*! While you were picking out a training bra or dreaming about getting a really cool tattoo some day, did you have even a clue what you would be doing for a living? There are people in their twenties and thirties still trying to pick out a career track and others in their forties changing from one career to another, either voluntarily or via the pink slip. Your government, however, *requires* 8th graders to make this choice so it can neatly allocate them into quotas for a Soviet-style workforce. What is the difference between Minnesota and Cuba in this regard? Nothing!

Don't worry, by the time your kid reaches 8th grade, he or she will have been so indoctrinated it won't matter what your expectations for them may be. Charlotte Thomson Iserbyt asks, "How can parents have a say in how their children are educated when the federal government is mandating testing of children's attitudes and values?"

Fully sixty percent of the test items on the National Assessment of Educational Progress (NAEP) are about *attitudes*! And you thought the government was testing to see if they had learned anything about history, literature, geography or science? Too late! What they have learned and what they are being tested for are the attitudes the government wants them to have. Not *yours*.

Writing in 1998, Lynne Cheney, an expert on education who is also the wife of our Vice President, pointed out the essential problem with the program described above, called "School to Work." The program, warned Cheney, doesn't "just direct job choices. They also inculcate attitudes." However, "predicting workforce needs is an iffy business." Thus, "redirecting schools to prepare students for jobs that central planners recommend does not guarantee the economic well-being of those students, and can even be a hindrance." Cheney added that "School to work materials frequently insist that all courses, even those in elementary school, relate to the world of work." This is right out of every five-year plan ever concocted by the former Soviet Russia.

This kind of government micro-management of what every child must learn runs contrary to the real goal of education which is to produce *good citizens capable of making their own choices*, having been provided with accurate information about American and world history, literature, science, geography, and the fundamentals of mathematics. This core education, available in the 1700s, 1800s, and early 1900s, produced generations of Americans who built this nation even if they literally studied by candlelight.

While you're being told that it's all about insuring children learn to read by a certain age or have good math and science skills, the real curriculum is about instilling government-approved attitudes about a range of topics that parents often find appalling. These include environmental, spiritual and sexual issues. The worst part of this is the fact that conservative Republicans, including Ronald Reagan, have gone along with this for decades. All but 33 Republicans voted for the new education bill. Its greatest cheerleader has been George W. Bush.

A still greater, more dangerous, intrusion between you and your child is the introduction of in-school health clinics that will deal with your child's physical and *mental* health. Don't expect them to ask for your input. Intimate physical exams are the order of the day and, if there's a bit too much energy, fidgeting, whatever, Jeannie or Johnny gets put on a regimen of Ritalin or some other mind-altering drug to keep them docile. Just try to stop this and you might find yourself in court for child abuse. What if they're sexually active? The clinic may just decide that condoms are the best answer. Same-sex preferences? That's okay too.

Doesn't anyone wonder why our schools have become places where kids now routinely shoot and kill their teachers and fellow students? Why are students engaging in sexual "experimentation" earlier and earlier? Why a black market in mind-altering drugs like Ritalin and Prozac has expanded to the schoolyards of America? Why our schools become such dangerous places to send our kids? Schools are beginning to resemble minimum-security prisons with metal detectors, security cameras, and required drug testing programs. None of this existed in the pre-1965 school systems throughout this nation.

The Bush/Kennedy program, called "Leave No Child Behind" was described by *The New York Times* as "a breathtaking intrusion of the federal government on state's control of education." Breathtaking, indeed. If the federal government controls the states' departments of education and your state controls your local board, that means you and the other parents have no say whatever. In reality, this massive program should be called "Leave no one alone."

And this has become a very costly enterprise. The property taxes of every homeowner keep going up and up in order to fund this education monopoly that appears to be answerable to no one.

Over the years, parents have been initially baffled when their kid comes home all stressed out about the rain forests or decides to become a vegetarian. We have a whole generation or two of brainwashed environmentalists because the schools have been turned into factories that turn them out like pop-tarts. Do they have a clue about real science? No. Do they have any grasp of geography? No. Can they spell? No. Do they know the difference between the Civil War and the Revolutionary War? No. But they *do* know that George Washington and Thomas Jefferson were "slave owners." They "know" a lot of things that just aren't true.

Their ignorance doesn't matter to the schools because it's not what they *know* that matters to the federal government and Education Establishment. It is what they *think*. It's whether they have been conditioned to trust Big

Brother and do whatever Big Brother says. *That's why the testing is so vital.* And, please, don't talk to me about school choice. All schools, public and private, are going to teach the same curriculum to achieve the same *required* results. Otherwise those federal dollars go bye-bye. That's what happens when the federal government controls the schools instead of local communities!

Do you ever wonder why home-schooled children consistently do better academically than those passing through this mind-numbing system? It's because they concentrate on the basics, on facts, on multiplication tables, on spelling things correctly, on learning how to express themselves, not to please Big Brother, but to please their parents.

Until the 1960's this was the way most schools taught children. After that, the "change agents" took over, transforming the children so they would be ready for a world without borders run by a megalith called the United Nations. Who created the UN? Soviet diplomats aided by members of the U.S. Department of State, all but one of whom was later found to be a member of the Communist Party USA and a secret agent.

Is this all part of some plot or conspiracy? Certainly, Charlotte Thomson Iserbyt's book (over 500 pages) documents the relationship between Soviet-style education and the one that has been slowly imposed on the United States. Others argue that it is simply the result of the juggernaut of an increasingly powerful Education Establishment based on a mandatory system, a monopoly that has tapped into federal tax dollars. The problem remains the same. Parents have few real choices at this point other than to educate their children at home if they wish to avoid what everyone, including many concerned educators, agree is a failed system.

Smarter, Better & Home Schooled!

As each school year begins or ends, I am reminded of the story of a boy whom the teachers complained about, saying he could not learn, seemed confused, and asked too many questions. Today, that boy would have been required to take Ritalin or some other drug. In his case, however, his parents decided to home school him. He was Thomas Edison.

Home schooling worked then and it works today. In fact, home schooling works far better than the deliberate stupifying of the children passing through what is surely the most expensive and ineffective educational system the world has ever known.

The American public education system today is not about educating students; it is about indoctrinating them. It has less to do with imparting information and more to do with instilling politically correct attitudes. It is producing docile, ignorant people who know little about their nation's history. This is imperceptibly—and some say deliberately—weakening our society.

Right now in America, public school enrollment is projected to reach a record 47.3 million and peak at 47.5 million by 2005. Private schools had 5.3 million students in the 1999-2000 school year. By contrast, between 1.6 and 2 million students were home schooled in the U.S. during 2001-2002, taking in every grade level from kindergarten through twelfth grade. There is, though, a surprise in that number. It is an increase of 500 percent over the number being home schooled a decade ago! The growth rate of the choice to home school is estimated to be between seven and fifteen percent each year.

In numbers, home schooled children are a minority among those being shuttled through elementary, middle and high schools like so much sausage. However, when they are in competition with the products of those public schools, they leave them way behind. The headlines tell the story. Put them in a spelling or geography bee and the home schooled child usually takes top honors. It's actually news when they do not!

Home schooled students in the U.S. score 15 to 30 percentile points, on average, above their school peers whether the subject is reading, writing, mathematics or science or social studies. The mediocre science scores of public school students were front-page news in January. In May, the news that most U.S. high school seniors had a poor grasp of their nation's history was also on the front pages. Diane Ravich, historian and education professor at New York University called the scores "abysmal." Bad as the scores were, they had shown no improvement since 1994!

Despite this obvious problem, President Bush signed an education bill, dubbed "Leave No Student Behind", that allocated $49 billion to a system so broken, so useless, that is a national shame and a national sham. His answer? Testing, testing, testing. But! If you are testing only the knowledge that is mandated for the test, all the ancillary knowledge needed to actually understand the subject is jettisoned for the sake of the test score.

Currently, the U.S. is spending about 72 percent more on education than in 1980. After more than two decades, there is no indication of any significant improvement. Instead, this huge investment of U.S. tax dollars has produced poor reading and other subject scores, static dropout rates, declining parental satisfaction, and mediocre U.S. student performance in international education surveys.

The home schooled student, notes Phyllis Schlafly, doesn't have to study "fuzzy math, whole math, new math, new new math, or rainforest math." They don't have to be taught "Whole Language, which fraudulently teaches children to guess at words from the pictures, skip over difficult words, and substitute any words that seem to fit the context."

In the fall of 1999, Ridgewood, NJ students, aged 11 to 18, were required to answer questions about their own drug use, sexual life, and any illegal activity in which they had been involved. The 156-question survey asked students to name how many times they had tried to kill themselves, used contraception, or made themselves throw up after eating. Parents took the school system to court and, after a two-year battle, won a victory for the First, Fifth, Fourth and Fourteenth Amendments.

Need it be said that none of the questions being asked had a single thing to do with whether the students had actually *learned* anything? Today's schools are about attitudes and behavior, not facts and skills.

Specious Science in Our Schools

Each September, millions of America's school children will return to their classrooms where their textbooks are teaching an utterly polluted stream of environmental and other science misinformation. Like so many issues involving our debased educational system, this is not evoking much public outcry. It should.

In January 2001, the Associated Press reported that "Twelve of the most popular science textbooks used at middle schools nationwide are riddled with errors, a new study has found." The study compiled 500 pages of errors!

"These are terrible books, and they're probably a strong component of why we do so poorly in science," said John Hubisz, the North Carolina State University physics professor who led the two-year study. He estimated that 85 percent of the nation's school children used the textbooks examined.

In November 2001, *USA Today* headlined an article, "Tests show U.S.

Alan Caruba

Students are weaklings in science." It was the usual litany of statistics adding up to the fact that about two-thirds of U.S. students have "a basic understanding of grade-level science, but only one-third or less can be considered proficient." This is a nice way of saying that, as in every other area of academics, the U.S. educational system is failing to teach yet another generation anything of value regarding science.

Rod Paige, the Secretary of Education, noted this abysmal level of science education undermines America's economic strength and security. "Instead of improving our own science education, we have been relying on the education of other countries provide to their citizens." In other words, the United States of America is forced to import our scientists, engineers and doctors.

I recently received a rant about a Ford Motor Company program that supports good science in the classroom. Ford had previously tried to ingratiate itself with the environmental movement. Belatedly realizing it had allied itself with people who hated cars, trucks and anything else that utilized petroleum products, Ford came to its senses. One can only wish other U.S. corporations would as well.

When John F. Borowski, a marine and environmental science teacher, emailed me his screed denouncing the Ford Motor Company for donating $1.5 million to underwrite a program called "Provider Pals," offering information about the way American industries extract natural resources or provide food, his name rang a bell.

On August 21, 1999, Borowksi had an opinion editorial published in *The New York Times* titled "Schools with a Slant." He decried "corporatism" claiming that public schools "are ripe for exploitation via dubious 'educational materials'" adding that it was not environmental groups that were intent on creating "ecowarriors," but rather it was "the business world that was "eager to turn our children into the ultimate consumers." Apparently, it has yet to have dawned on him that we live in a consumer society and that goods and the money spent on them have given us our extraordinary lifestyle, affording us the longest life expectancy in our nation's history.

Let us understand that people who harbor a hatred for corporations are, quite simply, socialists or even communists. It is corporate America, along with our countless small businesses, that generate the trillions that make our economy the greatest in the history of mankind. Where socialism exists, economies falter and stagnate, and people suffer.

In his latest diatribe, titled *Bastion of Ecological Literacy Under Siege:*

Our Public Schools, Borowski rants about Bruce Vincent, "an outspoken defender of logging, mining, and grazing on public lands" for creating a program that explains the role that loggers, miners, and ranchers play in providing the most essential resources this nation and its people require.

"It was the likes of Boise Cascade and Weyerhaeuser who butchered millions of acres of watersheds," says Borowski. No, it was the unrelenting refusal of environmental groups to permit the proper management of our national forests that led to the catastrophic loss by fire of millions of acres of timber. Starting with the Spotted Owl hoax and then suing every time a strand of forest was to be culled properly, the eco-maniacs like Borowski did more damage than all the timber companies combined.

Scott Blandish is an environmental science teacher in suburban Spokane, Washington who has written on the politicization of environmental curricula. "Kids are being terrorized in school every day with environmental nightmare stories about global warming, rising seas, desertification, (and) killer smog," Blandish told CNSnews.com in May 2000.

There are good science teachers and then there are the Borowski's whose only reason for teaching is the indoctrination of their students, filling their heads with environmental mush while fulminating against the evil "corporations" of America. As he says, "Corporate America knows as long as students have literacy in environmental issues, there will always be Rachel Carson and Cesar Chavez.

Thanks to Carson, millions have died from malaria, deprived of the protection DDT once provided. Strange heroes for a world that must feed six billion people and protect them from Nature's predators.

Every Sunday, my local daily newspaper publishes letters from school children throughout northern New Jersey and, every week for years, some child is worried about global warming, forests, water, oil, the ozone layer, endangered species.

These children and millions of others who have passed through the schools of our nation have had their perceptions of the real world, of Nature, perverted by the textbooks and curricula of their so-called science classes.

In science classes, in courses about history, civics, and throughout the perverted curriculum of our nation's schools, our children are being indoctrinated, not educated, to hate America, its economic system, and its values.

Alan Caruba

The Subversion of Education in America

A Four-Part Series

The Subversion of Education in America: Lesson #1

I'll bet you think that the problems with our nation's schools are a fairly recent phenomenon. Wrong. It dates backs to the 1960's. Those that have implemented the subversion of our educational system have sought to fly well below the radar of public awareness, depending on stealth and duplicity to achieve the wreckage that has already stunted the lives of thousands who have passed through it.

No other topic has evoked as much email as did our weekly "Warning Signs" commentary, "Indoctrination, Not Education." Good. Time to wake up America!

In this and three other commentaries, I will walk you through the history of the problem with the help of an extraordinary book, *The Deliberate Dumbing Down of America* by Charlotte Thomson Iserbyt. The facts I will share with you are found in a fat compendium of research by this former senior official with the U.S. Department of Education who discovered the mother lode, copied it, and fled. She is one of America's unsung heroes.

As Iserbyt points out, in the 1960's "American education would henceforth concern itself with the importance of the *group* rather than with the importance of the individual." The purpose of education would shift to focus on the student's *emotional* health, rather than academic learning. Remember the 1960's? Sex, drugs and rock'n roll? Drop out, tune in, and turn on? Just about everything that is wrong with America today had its genesis in this pathetic decade of youthful self-indulgence."

In 1965, there were two major federal initiatives developed with funding from The Elementary and Secondary Education Act passed that year. One was the 1965-1969 Behavioral Science Teacher Education Program and the other was the publication by the government of *Pacesetters in Innovation*, a 584-page catalogue of behavior modification programs to be used by the schools.

Let me repeat that: a catalogue of *behavior modification* programs!

56

We're not talking of programs to teach students anything. We are talking about programs to indoctrinate children passing through the system to believe in values contrary to those on which this nation was based.

In brief, the intention was to create a generation or two of Americans who would accept the United Nations, not the United States, as their new "nation," a global nation, one-world government. The last thing the conspirators wanted was a nation of individuals who could or would actually think for themselves. This is how we ended up with Bill Clinton, the classic student achiever of the 1960s.

Iserbyt writes that, "In 1960, the United Nations Educational, Scientific and Cultural Organization's Convention Against Discrimination was signed in Paris. This convention laid the groundwork for control of American education—both public and private—by UN agencies and agents."

Now connect the dots. In 1960, *Soviet Education Programs: Foundations, Curriculums, Teacher Preparation* was published under the auspices of the U.S. Department of Health, Education and Welfare. It was the blueprint for the U.S. school-to-work restructuring that would take place and it would rely on the "Pavlovian conditioned reflex theory." The mastermind of mind control and conditioning was a psychologist, Dr. B.F. Skinner who was the guru of the mess that passes for education in America today.

Though hard to believe even now, the U.S. adopted the Soviet Communist approach to education. In 1961, Rep. John M. Ashbrook tried to alert Congress to what was happening. Citing a document published by the Department of Health, Education and Welfare called *A Federal Education Agency for the Future,* he called the new education programs "a blueprint for complete domination and direction of our schools from Washington." Guess what? He was right.

That is why the educational reform this nation really needs is the complete elimination of the U.S. Department of Education. It won't happen. For the same reason we are now only learning that those "Red baiters" of the 1950's were right to assert the Department of State was shot through with Communists, no one in 2001 is going to believe that the U.S. Department of Education is modeled on Communist theories.

The Subversion of Education in America: Lesson #2

Just how did education in America turn from being a system that imparts knowledge to one that uses behavior modification techniques to influence the attitudes and beliefs of those passing through it?

To achieve this, beginning in the 1960's, the perpetrators of the subversion have employed deception to achieve their goals. Earlier this month, a New Jersey daily newspaper ran an editorial, "Let board members speak," noting that members of a local school board had been restricted from speaking to the press to avoid "confusion" about the board's programs and objectives. "But this isn't about 'confusion'," said the editorial. "It's about control," adding "And it is insulting to the public and the idea of open local government."

There is nothing "open" about the effort to subvert education in America. It only has that appearance because it takes place at presumably local school boards or in a state education department. Always, the vehicle is a governmental agency. The controlling player, however, is the U.S. Department of Education.

The objective of those who control our educational systems has long been to produce poorly educated, little world citizens, ready to forego the liberties guaranteed by the oldest living Constitution. The system introduced into American schools mirrors the Soviet and Communist Chinese systems that produce a compliant and complacent population.

To achieve this, they have had to dumb-down the students passing through the system. On February 17, 2001, the *Los Angeles Times* reported that the president of the University of California "wants to eliminate the SAT as a requirement for admission to all eight of the university's undergraduate campuses." What a great way to further dilute all standards for academic achievement!

In January 2001, the *Times* reported that the University of California kicked out 2,009 students, six percent of last year's freshman class, for failing to master basic math and English skills in their first year of classes. These are skills that *should have been mastered* in their first twelve years in California schools! It means that the diplomas they received are *worthless pieces of paper.*

This pattern repeats itself from state to state because it is the educational *system* that is failing American students. The President's emphasis on testing misses the point entirely!

In the January/February 2001 issue of *The American Enterprise*, devoted to why some few schools succeed while the majority fail, Karl Zinsmeister writes that "it's extremely interesting how many common traits are shared by the successful schools we profile. A remarkably similar basic formula applies in almost all of these places: high demands on students, strict discipline, a strong and unapologetic moral component, including a respect for religion, an emphasis on teaching intellectual basics, a preference for time-tested books and curricula, clear standards of dress, grooming, and comportment, and an insistence on politeness, respect and courtesy."

Compare that to schools in your area where the way students dress is an offense to decorum, the language they use is replete with profanities, and their chief complaint is that they have too much homework.

President Bush has bought into the Education Establishment's systematic stupification of students. He is not the first President to fall prey to this effort. To learn the facts, you must read *The Deliberate Dumbing Down of America* by Charlotte Thomson Iserbyt.

The President has proposed a five billion-dollar program to help children learn to read. Please! Please, please, will someone explain to me why spending even *more* money will answer the question of why our schools, soaking up billions a year, are NOT teaching this already?

One need only look at the realities of education in Texas to see why the call for national testing standards is a deception. An excellent article by Jerry Jesness in the November 2000 issue of *Reason* magazine blows away the hype about the test scores of Texas students. Despite apparent improvements, a closer look at the test scores of basic skills places young Texans in 39th place for SAT scores.

In 1984, the State adopted the Texas Educational Assessment of Minimal Skills that established minimal standards for graduation. The result has been that a considerable amount of time is spent "teaching to the test" in schools throughout Texas. Students are taught strategies to pass the text. For example, the acquisition of real arithmetical skills is sacrificed to methods that include drawing and counting sticks! This is not progress and the test is, essentially, meaningless.

All this was foretold back in the 1970's as the "educrats" continued their efforts to undermine the teaching of basic knowledge. In 1976, Catherine Barrett, then president of the National Education Association, gave a speech in which she said, "First, we will help all of our people understand that school is a concept and not a place. We will not confuse "schooling" with education. The school will be the community, the community the school." This predates Hillary Clinton's "it takes a village" concept, but it reflects a communist view that all of society must be employed to form the views of students. Individualism is bad. Conforming to the group is good.

Barrett went on to say "We will need to recognize that so-called 'basic skills' which currently represent nearly the total effort in elementary schools, will be taught in *one quarter* of the present school day. The remaining time will be devoted to what is truly fundamental and basic— time for academic inquiry, time for students to develop their own interests, time for a dialogue between students and teachers...more than a dispenser of information, the teacher will be a conveyor of values, a philosopher. Students will learn to write love letters and lab notes."

You may want to read this again. The then-head of the NEA was talking about turning the school day into one devoted to just about everything *other* than the teaching of reading, writing and arithmetic. Teachers were, instead, to become "agents of change."

The change incorporated into today's educational programs is intended to change the *entire social structure of our society* and the values that had made it great. Competition and achievement in the acquisition of basic knowledge and the skills to implement that knowledge are jettisoned in favor of changing attitudes about family, patriotism, religion, and sexuality. Look around you and ask yourself why we now except all forms of "families." Look around you and ask why we live in a cultural environment drenched with sexuality without responsibility. Ask yourself why millions fail to vote. Look at the way the expression of religious values is continually derided.

In 1972, Dr. Chester M. Pierce, MD, of Harvard University wrote an article entitled "Becoming Planetary Citizens: A Quest for Meaning" that appeared in the November issue of *Childhood Education*. He was concerned that children, by the age of five, "already have a lot of political attitudes," among which were "a tenacious loyalty to his country and its leader." What he wanted was a child who entered kindergarten "with the same kind of loyalty to *the earth* as to his homeland..."

This is a formula for degrading patriotism and loyalty to everything for which this nation stands in favor of creating citizens of the "global government" being pursued by the United Nations and the environmentalism that preaches against the use of the earth's natural resources.

All throughout the 1970s, the Federal government funded these goals.

Local educational systems were taken over by programs designed to destroy local control. I do not want President Bush's education proposals to succeed because they reflect the continued subversion of our nation's schools by the Department of Education.

The process dates back to the 1960s, continued through the 1970's, and in the following discussion of education in America, we will see how they increased through the 1980s.

The Subversion of Education in America: Lesson #3

This will come as a surprise to you—everything about the nation's educational system does—but Congress back in 1970 recognized that the federal government is supposed to have limited authority when it comes to education. An amended General Education Provisions Act specifically articulated a "prohibition" against federal control of education.

It forbids the federal government from exercising any "direction, supervision, or control over the curriculum, program of instruction, administration or personnel of any education institution, school, or school system, or over the selection of library resources, textbooks, or other printed or published instructional materials by any educational institution or school system."

The loophole through which the subversion of our education system was accomplished was federal funding of "research" and "development."

By the 1980s (see the previous two editions of "Warning Signs" for a look at the 1960s and 1970s by clicking on the Archives below) the effort to turn schools from places where students actually learn something to places where their values, beliefs, and cognitive skills were determined by "Outcome Based Education," behavior modification programs. The objective of these programs is to turn students in to little citizens of a one-world government where they are mere economic units, not individuals, nor people who give much thought to individual liberty.

Individual liberty was the reason the American Revolution was fought and is the philosophical basis for every word in the U.S. Constitution. A generation or two of Americans who are systematically robbed of any knowledge of this are ripe for an authoritarian takeover.

The father of this movement is Prof. Benjamin Bloom and his book, *All Our Children learning*. Published in 1981, it is the bible of OBE. In it he says, "The purpose of education and the schools is to change the thoughts, feelings, and actions of students." No, the purpose of education is to provide students with a sufficient knowledge of basic skills in writing, reading, arithmetic, as well as history and the sciences. Thus prepared, they are likely to be the kind of citizens that will question efforts to deprive this nation of its sovereignty in favor of a world government run out of the United Nations.

It gets worse. Writing in *The Effective School Report*, Dr. Thomas A. Kelly, Ph.D., stated that "The brain should be used for processing, not storage." This is the view of education that says you prepare students to take a test determined by federal standards of what they should know. The student is merely to *process* predetermined bits and pieces of information. The best example of this is the rat's maze where the rat learns to follow a specific path to get a piece of cheese.

This is a simplified explanation of why today's children have difficulty acquiring and retaining a body of useful, long-term information such as multiplication tables or who the nation's presidents have been, the 50 States of the Union, when the Civil War was fought, where India can be found on a map, the names of the earth's oceans, et cetera!

The whole movement to utterly change the direction and purpose of our nation's schools picked up momentum in the 1980's and, sorry to say it, it occurred on Ronald Reagan's watch. The harsh truth about the subversion of the nation's schools has not been a Democratic or Republican program. It has occurred no matter who was in office or who controlled Congress. It happened because few politicians were paying any attention to what was really occurring over at the Department of Education.

In her book, *The Deliberate Dumbing Down of America*, Charlotte Thompson Iserbyt, says, "The real purpose of this project was to propose a radical redesign of the nation's education system from one based on inputs to one based on outputs." It switched, in other words, from a curriculum of *content* a student was required to learn, to *a series of answers* the student was supposed to repeat when tested. Or as Iserbyt explains it, the system turned away "from one oriented toward the learning of *academic content* to one based on performance of *selected skills*, necessary for the implementation of school-to-work ..." The schools, with direction from the DOE and grants from major foundations, as well as input from corporate leaders, were redesigned to produce workers.

Well, what's so bad about that? We need workers. Ask anyone responsible for the management of any size organization, from a local bakery to a major corporation, what their primary problem is and they will tell you it's finding good workers. That is to say, finding people with even the most basic education or skills to perform any job with a minimum of competency. That is the result of the education system that has been foisted on this nation.

Take away their pocket calculators and the newest generation of workers cannot add or subtract. Take away "spell check" on their computers and they are helpless to spell accurately. These are basic skills Americans used to learn in one-room schoolhouses heated with a wood-burning oven. They could also tell you the branches of the U.S. government and a whole lot more than today's graduates.

In the 1980's the DOE says Iserbyt, "effectively transformed the essential character of the nation's public schools from 'teaching'—the most traditional and conservative role of schools—to 'workforce training'—perceived as liberal and 'progressive.'" It is a particular irony that one of Ronald Reagan's campaign platforms was the abolishing of the Department of Education. He was right. He didn't do it.

What, in fact, happened was that control of the schools and their curriculums increasing moved up the decision-making ladder away from local school boards and even state education departments. Administrators and teachers were delighted with this because it eliminated the "meddling" of locally elected and locally responsible school board members.

The instrument for this was the development of a "Course Goals Collection" completed by the DOE in 1980-81. "The collection consists of fourteen volumes with 15,000 goals covering every major subject taught in the public schools from K-12." Remember that 1970 prohibition on any federal government involvement in instruction? Nobody else did either.

In 1981, 70,000 copies were distributed, despite the fact that only approximately 16,000 school districts existed. And you wonder why every state now has the same goals? With remarkable success, Outcome-Based Education became the way American students were to be trained to believe the same things, have the same values, and to ignore those they were taught at *home*.

This is important because values are supposed to be the job of parents. Some parents are Catholic. Some parents are Protestant. Some are Jewish or Muslim. Some are liberal and some are conservative. Their values no longer seem to matter. That's why there no longer is a moment of prayer in any school in America. That's why the school day often does not begin with the salute to the flag or a recitation of a pledge of allegiance. Much of the day is spent "teaching to the test" whose standards were determined in Washington, D.C., not by the parents, not by the local school board, not by anyone *you* know!

How was this achieved? Because, according to a 1981 report by the Office of Educational Research and Improvement, "Federal funds account for approximately ten percent of national expenditures on education. The Federal share of educational research and related activities, however, is *ninety percent* of the total national investment."

Thus, as Iserbyt notes in her book, "just about everything that goes on in the classrooms of American public schools, with the exception of salaries, school buildings, buses, and the purchase of equipment, is either a direct or indirect result of funding by the U.S. Department of Education— as research!"

It should come as no surprise that, by the end of the 1980's, writing in the January 25, 1989 issue of *Education Week*, Chester E. Finn, Jr., the former head of the DOE's research branch, would tell business leaders that he favored a "national curriculum." Flashback to the congressional prohibition on a curriculum determined at the federal level. Consider it null and void. The people in the DOE obviously did.

Little wonder, too, that in 1989, then-President George H. Bush unveiled "America 2000" (now known as "Goals 2000") to the National Governor's Association that virtually set in concrete the whole behavior modification movement that has been foisted on the American education system.

That same year, the Association for Supervision and Curriculum Development's *Elementary Global Education Framework* was announced. Its goals were to create "Human beings whose home is planet earth, who are citizens of a multicultural democratic society in an increasingly interconnected world, and who learn, care, think, choose, and act, to celebrate life on this planet, and to meet the global challenges confronting Humankind."

NO! We are talking about AMERICAN students going to AMERICAN schools in the sovereign nation of the UNITED STATES OF AMERICA. We are not sending kids to school to become citizens of the world, programmed to deal with global challenges, i.e., threats to the environment that require we all cut back on the use of energy or pick up the bill to bring developing nations up to speed. That is exactly the game plan of the United Nations and the worldwide conspiracy of socialists masquerading as environmentalists.

That is, however, what is going on in our schools TODAY. That's why President George W. Bush's proposal to throw $5 billion at those schools, presumably to teach a subject, reading, *they should already be teaching*, is a continuation of the same bad ideas that president's since Eisenhower have been rubber-stamping. And then ignoring.

The Subversion of Education in America: Lesson #4

I have lived my whole life in an affluent, suburban community in Northern New Jersey. When I attended its schools in the 1940's and 1950s, the vast percentage of graduating seniors went onto college. Their parents had migrated from Newark during or just after WWII because the schools had an excellent reputation. Today, they are not much better than those of the inner city.

Here's an excerpt from a letter to the editor in our local weekly. "I understand that our education officials have yet to detail for the public exactly what measures have been taken to ensure that a first-rate education will be provided for students." This stonewalling is endemic to education bureaucrats across the nation. He thinks he's going to get an answer. He won't.

"I was horrified to learn that 34 percent of the eighth grade students in (our) Middle School were found only partially proficient—the worst grouping—in the 2000 GEPA math section. Simply put, we rank 97th out of 97 schools in this failing category. Further, this dreadful performance has been repeated over the past several years.

"As a homeowner and a taxpayer, I want to know how the district's school budget increased from $51 million five years ago to $70 million today, a 37 percent increase over four years, during which time these poor test scores have not gotten measurably better and our last place ranking has not moved out of the cellar."

Throwing more and more money at our nation's current education system is not the answer. The system is inherently flawed because it is not intended to provide a basic 3R's education.

President Bush proposes to introduce a national educational standard and then test to it, but *we already know* American students are deficient in all the areas of knowledge the schools are *supposed* to be teaching. The tests today's students take are more about their values than about any body of knowledge they have acquired. Today's schools are not about educating students. They are about teaching attitudes and values.

If you have been reading my series over the past three commentaries in this series, you already know that the system has been designed to deliberately dumb down students.

The architects of this attack on our nation's youth can be found in the U.S. Department of Education. They have adopted psychological methods of conditioning and jettisoned the teaching of information and basic skills. It is called "Outcome-Based Education."

Today's students, as opposed to their grandfather's or even their father's education, are being systematically conditioned to think in "global" terms about humanity, nations, religions, and, of course, the environment. They are conditioned to be citizens, not of the United States, but of the world. That's what you need when you're creating a socialist one-world governmental system and that is exactly what is occurring at the United Nations.

Today's students are taught not to make value judgements about other nations, even if they are authoritarian dictatorships. They may not know where Brazil is on the map, but they "know" all the rain forests are disappearing. They don't know when the Civil War took place or why, but they "know" that all the Founding Fathers were slave-owners. They also "know" that America's history is one of destroying the native Indian nations, taking their land, and exploiting it with farms, mining, and the destruction of whole forests. They cannot tell you what the Bill of Rights is, but they "know" the U.S. is the leading contributor of "greenhouse gases" to the atmosphere, thereby causing global warming. It is a full course of lies.

They haven't a clue about the individualism, sacrifice, daring and innovation that made this nation great, nor its political system, and most certainly not its history.

As Charlotte Thompson Iserbyt writes in her book, *The Deliberate Dumbing Down of America*, they aren't been "taught the difference between free enterprise and planned economies, i.e., socialism; between 'group thinking' and individual freedom and responsibility."

By the 1990's the decades of effort to overturn an education system that taught specific bodies of information and the skills to use them—arithmetic, spelling, history, civics, science—had effectively been transformed into today's touchy-feely system. It is a place where a student's feelings of self-esteem are more important than whether they actually *know anything* other than the specific answers to the test. Thus teachers now "teach to the test" (their paycheck depends on it) rather than provide a broader body of knowledge. It is a place where competition is discouraged as unfair to those less qualified for any reason. It is a place where socialist attitudes and values are the priority, *not knowledge*.

Given President George W. Bush's enthusiasm for education that is "accountable" and "will leave no child behind," will it surprise anyone that the "America 2000 Plan," written in 1991, was presented to the American people by Lamar Alexander, the Secretary of Education serving his father, President George Herbert Walker Bush?

The "America 2000 Plan" proposed to radically restructure American society, beginning with its schools. It was intended to affect 11,000 public and private schools. When you're trying to create good little socialists, you can't afford to have anyone who is being taught to think *independently* or asked to incorporate *moral and ethical* values.

The "voucher" program exists to give the federal government control over private schools because, whoever pays the piper, chooses the tune. Schools that accept voucher students will soon find themselves required to accept federal education regulations as well.

"Goals 2000" and "School-to-Work" programs introduced to transform our schools reflect what Iserbyt describes as "the internationalization of education with exchanges of data systems, curricula, methods, et cetera, all essential for the implementation of the international socialist management and control system being put in place right now."

Everything, including the SAT college entrance tests, has been degraded to mask the dumbing down those who are passing through our schools. Today's SATs permit students to use electronic calculators, ask fewer questions in general and fewer multiple-choice math questions in particular. Reading passages now ask definitions from context and the formerly difficult antonym section, calling for linguistic and intellectual subtleties, has been dropped entirely.

My hometown's parent who could not get any answers from his district's school board could not know that this is repeated across America in school after school. Parents are routinely lied to. Worse, today's parents are often required to put their child put on a regimen of Ritalin, a mind-altering drug. We've got seven million *government-approved drug addicts* going to school in drug-free zones!

To the individual parent, there seems to be no way to resist the juggernaut of a system that routinely turns out thousands of "educated" morons. Some choose to home-school their children. Others who can afford it send them to private schools. Still others shell out for after-school tutoring services. Why? Because the schools have been "restructured."

President Bush is *not* providing a solution. He is *part* of the problem. His father was part of the problem. Presidents going back to Eisenhower have been part of the problem because they failed to see that introducing Soviet-style educational methods—*behavior modification to produce good little socialists*—into American schools was destined to bring us to this point.

Education is *not* about national standards and national testing. It's about individual schools in individual school districts, all answerable to their communities and to the parents of the children entrusted to them. It's not about how the child *feels*, but about how well the child *learns*. There is pride in learning, but if there are no grades, how does anyone, parent, child or teacher know what, if anything, is being learned?

Congress will probably give President Bush the $5 billion he wants to throw away on failed reading programs, and money for the national educational standards and testing he wants. Previous Congresses have gone along, failing or refusing to see how the educational system has been corrupted. The Republican "Contract with America" and the campaign promise of Ronald Reagan to dismantle the Department of Education had it right. It didn't happen. It is the only hope to reverse the damage and return schools to local control.

Sit down with your child and watch "Jeopardy" together. If neither you, nor your child knows the answer to anything other than the television or film questions, you're in trouble. Now multiply that against an entire population of Americans who don't know the answers either.

Animal "Rights"

Just How Crazy Are They?

In an "open letter" to *Vegan Voice*, a publication for vegetarians, Karen Davis of United Poultry Concerns, wrote "In conclusion, I think it is speciesist to think that the September 11 attack on the World Trade Center was a greater tragedy than what millions of chickens endured that day and what they endure every day because they cannot defend themselves against the concerted human appetites arrayed against them."

Yes, you read it correctly. Ms. Davis is comparing the lives of more than 3,000 men and women who died in that attack to the lives of CHICKENS.

She goes on. "Perhaps the word 'tragedy' should not be used anyway in this context unless in the more precise sense of a fundamentally terrible thing happening to a human being who consciously or subconsciously brought the terrible thing upon him or herself, lived through it, and gained insight and wisdom as a result. In a classic sense of tragic drama, it remains to be seen whether America is a 'tragic hero' or even a 'tragic' victim."

This soulless protector of chickens is asserting that the most important thing about the September 11th attack is not a tragedy for those who died, those family and friends who survived them, and the nation as a whole. She even suggests that they may have brought the attack upon themselves because they showed up for work that day. Or they responded to the scene and gave their lives trying to save others. Then she questions whether America is a victim of the worst act of terrorism ever perpetrated against

69

this nation.

"If though, the question is whether the World Trade Center attack was worse for its thousands of human victims than the sum total of misery and terror it was for millions of chicken victims that day, I see only one nonspeciesist answer to the question."

If you'd like to tell Ms. Davis the difference between killing humans and killing chickens, you can write her at United Poultry Concerns, PO Box 150, Machipongo, VA 23405 or email her at Karen@UPC-online.org. For more information about this organization that cares more for chickens than humans, you can check it out at www.UPC-online.org.

It's worth noting that the 9-11 attack didn't deter the crazies who think that the lives of animals are equal to the lives of humans. Three days before the attack Animal Rights lunatics torched a McDonald's restaurant in Tucson, Arizona. Following the attack they set fire to a maintenance building at the primate research facility in New Mexico, released minks from an Iowa fur farm twice within a week, and firebombed a federal corral for wild horses in Nevada.

Federal authorities and State police are trying to determine if radical Greens were involved in placing two bombs that were found and disarmed at two forestry buildings on the Michigan Tech University campus in Houghton, Michigan.

Meanwhile, two environmental groups are suing the Bush Administration to block the removal of charred trees from a forest ravaged by fires last summer. The Wilderness Society and American Wildlands filed suit on December 18th to block the expediting of a timber-salvage program on 44,000 acres of the Bitterroot National Forest in Montana. If this sensible forest management effort is not undertaken, these charred trees will be nothing more than fodder for the next fire a bolt of lightning will ignite. What these two groups want, like all their Green brothers and sister, is to insure that our forests burn rather than be tainted by the use of human beings.

The Animal Liberation Front claimed credit for four of the attacks and the Earth Liberation Front took credit for attempted bombing. David Barbarash, a spokesman for both groups said that the September 11th attacks has changed nothing for these Green terrorists. Barbarash says that these animal rights and environmental gangsters aren't terrorists because their aim is not to harm people, but to protect animals and the environment. ALF and ELF are just terribly misunderstood because they "are acting out of compassion for all life, including human life."

Meanwhile, they go around destroying facilities that are engaged in invaluable medical research or which pursue commercial activities that include fur farming and private property such as the Vail Ski resort in an October 1998 fire.

In December, it was revealed that federal and state wildlife biologists had planted false evidence of a rare cat species in two national forests, the Gifford Pinchot National Forest and Wenatchee National Forest in Washington State. Had they gotten away with this despicable perversion of science, the evidence they planted would have led to the banning of various forms of recreation and use of these two forest areas.

As 2002 begins, the law enforcement and other agencies of the Federal government are focused on determining who among us poses a threat of militant Islam, but for decades now, Animal Rights and Greens have been engaged in a massive campaign of propaganda—lies—that have imposed bans, limitations, and increased costs on every aspect of our lives. Some have engaged in arson, break and entry, vandalism, and theft to advance their cause. In addition to the Islamic militants among us, we have a cadre of terrorists who need to be hunted and jailed before they become further emboldened to harm our lives and our nation.

Coyotes & Turkeys & Bears, Oh My!

Here are some headlines in the daily newspaper that serves my State. "Coyote pack gets too close for comfort." And "Hide Food: They're Up and Hungry." The latter is about bears. So, the coyotes, the bears, and, of course, the huge population of white-tailed deer continue to pose problems for my fellow residents of—would you believe this—New Jersey!

That's right. New Jersey; home to "The Sopranos," the gambling mecca of Atlantic City, the Garden State Parkway, the New Jersey Turnpike, the New Jersey Devils hockey team and, despite its designation as New York, the football Giants who play in our Meadowlands stadium. New Jersey, home to vast shopping malls, jam-packed cities, and lovely suburbs. It is the very epicenter of so-called "urban sprawl."

"Normally, most of the state's estimated 1,400 black bears awake from winter around the end of March, then survive in the woods on available plants like skunk cabbage", said the article in *The Star-Ledger*. "But in this year's unseasonably warm winter, more bears than usual have emerged

71

from hibernation a month early and have gone looking for food." And then comes this cautionary note, "That means the bears have gone roaming nearer to homes looking for food, authorities say."

In August 2002, a black bear killed a small child. The first such incident in modern memory, but a warning that it will not be the last.

As to the other critters, "A pack of coyotes have been seen running through residential areas of Denville in the past few weeks, alarming residents who once embraced the novelty of hearing the 'song dogs' howling at night." And get this! "The coyotes have killed wild turkeys, brought down deer, and, in at least one case reported two weeks ago, attacked domestic dogs on the south end of the township ..."

Here in New Jersey we are reading, once again, about coyotes, bears, wild turkeys, and, of course, the deer, the endless deer. Estimates range up to 170,000 deer with more each year. More than existed when the Lenni Lenapi Indians roamed these parts. Soon enough, there will be the usual spate of stories about the federally protected Canadian geese befouling parks, golf courses, and anywhere else people want to take a stroll.

I suggest, the next time someone tells you that these and other critters are "endangered," you punch them out. While they lay sprawled on the ground, you say, "You want endangered species, pal? Move to New Jersey. They're crawling with wildlife and it's in the suburbs, it's in the cities, it's everywhere including the many highways and byways where a collision with a white-tailed deer can get you severely dead."

We don't need to have nearly half the nation's landmass put aside as national parks, forests, and refuges to protect the poor "endangered" species. They are in our backyard. You don't have to worry about the spotted owls and the thousands of other creatures the Greens have had designated for the sole purpose of keeping you out of "their" habitat. They are in "our" habitat.

You do need to worry about Green members of the Fish and Wildlife Service, the Forest Service, the National Park Service, and other federal and state agencies falsifying "scientific evidence" to insure you will be kept out of those areas. Right now, this consists of 83,000,000 acres of National Parks and 191,000,000 acres of the National Forest System.

The next time you read of some politician trying to come up with yet another way to wrest privately owned property from some rancher, farmer, developer or homeowner—anywhere—they should be met with a crowd of torch-bearing protesters and given the message, keep your hands off our property!

The next time some federal agency tells you that you're forbidden to hike, hunt, fish, climb or use land put aside for the use of Americans, get out the torches and start marching. It's not the animals that are endangered; it's our constitutionally protected property rights.

Finally, need it be said that the human population has just as many rights, if not more, to the same habitat as the animals? We live on barely 3.5 percent of the entire land mass of the nation.

The Truth About the Animal Rights Movement

Here's a tip of the hat to my friend, Tom DeWeese, the president of the American Policy Center who provided the following quotes by leaders of the animal rights movement.

An Anti-Human Philosophy:

"I don't believe that people have the right to life. That's a supremacist perversion. A rat is a pig is a dog is a boy." – Ingrid Newkirk, co-founder and national director of PETA.

"Man is the most dangerous, destructive, selfish, and unethical animal on earth." – Michael Fox, vice president, Human Society of the United States

"Mankind is the biggest blight on the face of the earth." – Ingrid Newkirk, PETA.

"Six million people died in concentration camps, but six billion broiler chickens will die this year in slaughterhouses." – Ingrid Newkirk, PETA.

"An (animal) experiment cannot be justified unless the experiment is so important that the use of a brain-damaged human would be justifiable." – Peter Singer, professor, Princeton University

On Biomedical Research: "Even if animal tests produced a cure (for AIDS), we'd be against it." – Ingrid Newkirk, PeTA.

"If the death of one rat cured all diseases, it wouldn't make any difference to me." – Chris Rose, director, Last Chance for Animals.

"If it (the abolition of animal research) means there are some things we cannot learn, then so be it. We have no basic right not to be harmed by those natural diseases we are heir to." – Tom Regan, *America's New Extremists: What You Need to Know About the Animal Rights Movement.*

Immigration Issues

The Immigrant Tide: A High Risk Game

In 2002, there were more than 2,000,000 documents filed by immigrants, everything from 200,000 change of address forms, 300,000 applications for citizenship, to requests for benefits, sitting in a warehouse outside of Kansas City, Missouri. The Immigration and Naturalization Service (INS) has been unable to process them. Let us officially declare this government agency a disaster zone.

Let us also take notice that our immigration policies contributed to 9-11. Further, it should be stated that our immigration policies are putting pressures on this nation—its taxpayers—to function effectively, given that we are engaged in a war on terrorism while also having to maintain our educational and health systems, to name just two.

It is now a cliché that the failure to effectively screen foreign visitors, particularly Saudis, contributed to 9-11, but did you know that since then, 50,000 new visas have been granted to visitors from the Middle East and other nations that are home to Islamic extremists? The National Security Entry-Exit System, scheduled to begin in October, is intended to slow down the traffic in tourists and terrorists from the Middle East.

It will comfort to you to know that all those apply for visas must be reviewed by the Consular Lookout and Support System (CLASS) that utilizes information from the FBI, foreign governments, and other sources to determine if the applicant is a possible member of a terrorist organization, has a criminal record, et cetera.

75

Then, of course, there are the 5,000 terrorists that intelligence agencies estimate are already here; that number was reported by Bill Gertz in a July edition of the *Washington Times*. Of the investigations initiated by the FBI, so far only three men have been linked to al Qaeda. That leaves only 4,997 others to worry about.

The number of Middle Eastern immigrants represents a sevenfold increase over 1970. In that year, only 15 percent were Muslims. By 2000, an estimated 75 percent were Muslim. These immigrants set up their own Islamic schools and Daniel Pipes, director of the Middle East Forum, says that 80 percent of these schools, as well as their mosques and newspapers, subscribe to a militant version of Islam. There will be an estimated 2.5 million Muslims living in America by 2010. Says Pipes, "In its long history of immigration, the United States has never encountered so violent-prone and radicalized a community as the Muslims who have arrived here since 1965."

As if potential terrorists weren't a concern in itself, many of our nation's hospitals are feeling the financial burden of having to treat illegal immigrants. The U.S. Comptroller General David Walker of the General Accounting Office acknowledges that "hospitals are inundated with thousands of illegal immigrants seeking medical care." Who pays for it? David Ray, a spokesman for the Federation for American Immigration Reform (FAIR), correctly notes that "The only person getting the short end of the stick in this whole bargain is the taxpayer and disadvantaged Americans who rely on public health centers to stay alive." Illegal immigrants "are showing up for free health care and then going home." FAIR estimates that the national cost incurred by illegal aliens for Medicare and Medicaid is $3.7 billion. This especially affects border States with Mexico and others like Florida.

Immigration right now is a no-win situation for the United States that cries out for swift and major changes. There's the obvious issue of national security that is being ignored and then there are the costly financial pressures being put on our health, educational and criminal justice systems. The answer is a moratorium while this nation is in a virtual state of war with militant Islam and a wholesale invasion of illegals from Mexico.

The facts speak for themselves. The July 15 edition of *Insight* carried an article, "Immigration Surges in U.S." by Stephen Dinan. "The United States is accepting immigrants at a faster rate than any other time since the 1850s, according to Census 2000 figures release in June." The current 11.3 million foreign-born residents represent a 57 percent increase over figures from the 1990 Census.

Our borders, for all intents and purposes, do not exist. We are no safer today from terrorists than on September 11, 2001 and there is no political will, from the White House to Congress, to do anything about it. Worse, there are continuing legislative efforts to weaken our current immigration system.

Immigration, enshrined in our nation's history, has become a high-risk game that has already cost us the lives of more than 2,800 innocent people on 9-11 and may well cost many more. The failure to assert any control over our current immigration policies is costing U.S. taxpayers billions while undermining our health care and educational systems. Any way you look at it, this nation is in peril so long as nothing is done to correct the system and assert the inviolability of our borders.

Mexicans, Legal & Illegal, Transform U.S.

The 2000 Census revealed that, in at least 13 States surveyed to date, more U.S. residents are speaking Spanish at home. Not English. This is the result of nation's growing Hispanic population throughout the 1990s. It has risen an astonishing 58 percent to 35.3 million.

In some places such as California, native-born English-speaking business owners are taking Spanish lessons or hiring bilingual employees. Speaking Spanish at home is fine with me, but taking it out to the larger community and, in effect, requiring that it too speak Spanish is just dead wrong. A common language binds Americans to one another. Two languages in the same nation creates two separate communities.

The flow of illegal aliens from Mexico and nations further south is a virtual torrent. In the first six months of this year, the U.S. Border Patrol apprehended 176,655 illegal aliens in just the 21-mile Douglas, Arizona, section alone! The same individual may be apprehended more than once and the Border Patrol estimates that, for every one that is caught, *three to five* are not! Since 1983, at least a half-million illegal aliens have entered the U.S. from our southern border.

A study by the non-profit Center for Immigration Studies confirms that "annual immigration in 2030 will still approach 400,000 a year, 8.3 to 11.4 percent higher than the 370,000 estimated for 2000." The Mexican-born population of the United States will double to 18 million by the year 2030. There is a powerful incentive for this because, in the last decade, Mexican

77

immigrants sent more than $45 billion to their relatives. In 2000, they sent $6 billion or about $17 million a day!

Federal investigators recently revealed that "tens of thousands of foreigners are illegally obtaining Social Security numbers by using fake documents involving identity theft and other crimes. Federal officials have not yet found a way to search U.S. immigration records to prevent the practice. Using the Social Security identification, the next step is to secure credit cards and even security clearances that permit illegal aliens to work in sensitive areas such as airports. In 2001, the Social Security Administration issued 5.8 million numbers, including 1.5 million to non-citizens.

On May 5th, both the *Washington Post* and *Washington Times* reported that the families of eleven illegal immigrants who died while attempting to enter the United States had filed a $41 million lawsuit against two federal agencies. Allow me to provide my standard disclaimer. I do not dislike Mexicans. I don't even know a Mexican. If a Mexican has come here legally and become an American citizen, bravo! I have no problem with that, but the notion that the United States should be sued because it did not tend to the needs of those entering illegally is just nuts!

According to them, the failure of the United States, specifically the Department of Interior and the U.S. Fish and Wildlife Service, to provide water to Mexicans trying to sneak into America, was the reason they died. Their bodies were found last year in the Cabeza Prieta National Wildlife Refuge between Tucson and Yuma. That area was being used because, say the attorneys for the families, the U.S. Border Patrol has effectively shut down more populous portions of the Arizona border, thereby forcing illegal aliens to come in through more remote areas.

Well, it should be obvious that the U.S. is to blame, right? Why should we stop at providing water in a desolate desert where ground temperatures can exceed 130 degrees in the summer? Why not a fulltime bus service? Or chauffeured limousines? This Mexican version of an Alice in Wonderland approach to illegal immigration is why, in 1997, according to the Immigration and Naturalization Service, 54 percent of all illegal immigrants coming into the U.S. were Mexicans.

Could this be because elements of the Mexican *government* are carrying out a strategic depopulation program, centered around approximately ninety communities in central and southern Mexico? Some informed sources believe this to be the case. Making matters worse, according to Rep. Tom Tancredo (CO-R), since 1996 there have been 118 incursions across the border into the U.S.; 61 by Mexican military and 57 by Mexican law enforcement. At least 60 percent of the time, the Mexicans were armed. Sometimes U.S. Border guards come under fire.

The INS estimates that, in the past three years, more than a thousand migrants have died of various causes trying to enter the United States illegally. Their deaths, each one of them, were a tragedy, but it seems to me that it is a greater tragedy that Mexico does nothing to stem this human traffic. Maybe if Mexico took steps to improve its economy and provide jobs for its people, they would be working in Mexico instead of sneaking across the border?

And maybe President Bush's enthusiastic support for yet another amnesty program for illegal aliens is one of the dumbest ideas he's ever had? We are talking about adding another 200,000 illegal Mexican immigrants to the population. That's equivalent to adding a city the size of Baton Rouge, Bakersfield or Mobile. All this does is say to Mexicans that, if they can get into the U.S., they have a fair chance of going to the head of the line when the next amnesty comes. No need to apply for citizenship like others do. No need to come here, get a Green Card, and earn the right to be a citizen. Just sneak across the border.

Our immigration policies are so stupid that the House Judiciary Committee recently voted out Rep. Barney Frank's HR 1452, misnamed the Family Reunion Act, but in fact is legislation that would permit foreign criminals to stay in this country! It has 52 sponsors, most of whom are from the far Left of the Democrat Party, but that is not a long distance to traverse. The bill would erase the reforms achieved in the landmark 1996 immigration law requiring that, after serving their prison sentence here, they get deported.

This is why, at current rates, between legal and illegal immigration into this nation, we will *double* our population within the lifetimes of today's college students.

In the last decade, the 11.2 million immigrants who arrived, plus the 6.4 million children born to immigrants living here, equaled almost 70 percent of the nation's population growth. That's just flat-out too much, too fast.

Immigration Policies Transform
Europe's Politics

The mainstream press throughout America keeps viewing with alarm the transformation of Europe's politics, referring always to the growing concerns native-born Europeans have regarding that continent's immigration policies. This has given rise to "right-wing", i.e. conservative political parties.

Elections everywhere through Europe, including Great Britain, a member of the European Union, are putting a new breed of politician in office or providing strength in numbers for their parties. They vocally oppose immigration.

Everywhere, in Austria, France, Italy, Spain and other nations, the Socialist agenda of opening borders to immigrants, mainly from the Middle East and North African nations, is meeting with open resistance. Left-wing parties are losing power as Europeans grow weary of their rhetoric of "social justice." What people there are seeing is the loss of their national cultures and identities.

Europeans are seeing their social service systems fail under the burden of increasing immigration. They are seeing a rise in crime. The change has been relatively swift from the giddy days of the 1990s and earlier when Socialists gained power.

In England, a recent public opinion poll revealed that nearly half of those interviewed believe that immigration has damaged the nation over the past half-century. There is a protest against the construction of three new detention centers to deal with the influx of refugees. More than 72,000 people sought political asylum in Great Britain in 2001.

The British Home Secretary, David Blunkett, is heading to Paris to protest the failure of that nation to stem the flow of refugees through the rail tunnel that links England to France. Blunkett said that France "must accept that it cannot just tolerate thousands of illegal immigrants hanging around in northern France while they try and get into the United Kingdom." Immigration may just sweep the ruling Socialist Labor Party out of office in coming elections.

Socialists throughout Europe are facing a loss of power. This will directly impact on the European Union when upwards of fifteen member nations may soon have conservative governments forming a majority within a relatively short time.

The open door policy toward immigrants is likely to be transformed. This comes at a time when the economies of many European nations are sluggish, unemployment is high, and they are experiencing a growing older population. The irony is that many of these nations have relied on immigration to bolster their economies.

Across Europe, from Norway to Portugal to Austria, the tide is turning and it is turning on the issue of immigration. A lynchpin of this backlash is the growing population of Muslims throughout Europe. The European Union's support for the Palestinian Authority and its recent intervention to free thirteen terrorists who, among two hundred others, had seized the Church of the Nativity in Jerusalem, is causing alarm bells to go off among Europeans.

If it appears that the world is changing rapidly these days, it is. The grip that the former Soviet Union had on the politics of Eastern Europe has been broken. The appeal of Socialist politics and economics is waning in France, Germany, Italy and England, among others.

The vast flow of immigrants from Third World nations, many of them former European colonies, is going to slow. Those nations, in turn, will be forced to choose between fundamentalist Islam, corrupt and despotic leaders, and the decision to adopt the capitalist system that has brought prosperity to those nations that have long since passed through the Industrial Revolution and are into the Information Revolution.

Alan Caruba

The Islamic Jihad

The Middle East:
Where Trouble Lives and is Exported

(Editor's Note: This commentary was written in 2000, a year before 9-11, and in retrospect is prescient as well as a warning for the future.)

The Middle East "is progressively disengaging from the world economy," warns Patrick Clawson, an expert on the area. The region grew at only half the rate of other developing nations during the 1990s. The Middle East continues to slip further behind the West and even Asia. The Middle East today is a dangerous combination of poverty, a militant Islam, nationalism, and a mindset that blames everyone else for its problems.

I start with economics because so much of history comes down to nations going to war in order to gain more land, more resources, redress earlier losses, and generally trying to fatten their coffers with the riches of others. Vanity, envy and greed work in the lives of nations as they do in individuals. Ignorance, too.

Since 1948, Middle Eastern nations, rife with distrust for each other, have nonetheless been unified by the presence of the nation of Israel. It is not a Middle Eastern nation. It is a Western nation with Western values. As such, it is futile to think the other nations of the Middle East will ever made peace with it. A friend of mine who has been to the region many times and

83

spoken to both sides of the conflict says the mutual hatred is so intense that he would not now return for any reason.

Egypt's peace with Israel is little more than a realistic acceptance of the inability to defeat Israel in war. What they lost in war, the Sinai, was gained back for its promise of peace, but there is little peace in Egypt, occupied with maintaining its own fragile stability and kept afloat with massive foreign aid from the U.S.

From Iran to the tip of Yemen, none of the nations in that area can or will come to terms with Israel. For now, it is a convenient excuse for the autocratic leaders of Middle Eastern nations to maneuver for power, but most specifically, it is Iraq's Saddam Hussein ambition to rule the entire region.

Barely noticed, one of the first acts of the new Bush Administration in 2000 was to knock out rebuilt Iraqi radar stations. It was worth a minute on the evening news, but one no longer expects those who provide us news on television these days to grasp what is really occurring. When you combine the attention span of algae with a liberal knee-jerk response to every crisis, you get the nightly TV news.

The Middle East is a strange place to understand for most Americans and our European cousins. Despite having waged a losing war with Iran and then the Gulf War, Saddam Hussein's Iraq is widely seen as a "leader" throughout the Middle East. By some bizarre reverse psychology, Arabs are infatuated with the notion that the more you lose at war, the greater your stature is in that area of the world.

Back, briefly, to economics. There is little foreign investment in the Middle East due to a complete lack of confidence in the stability of the nations in that region. This can also be seen in the way the Middle East holds the largest share of wealth *abroad* with $350 billion collecting interest in banks *outside* the region. Since Islam forbids collecting interest, their banks can't let money make money, yet another roadblock to prosperity.

Despite the fact that OPEC's oil export revenue has risen from $99 billion in 1998 to $211 billion in 2000, the standard of living in the Middle East is atrocious. The average rate of population growth is second only to sub-Saharan Africa, a slim 2.2 percent during the last decade.

According to Freedom House, *five of the world's eleven most repressive countries are members of the Arab League.* Not one of the League's twenty-three members was found to extend any kind of freedom to their people. According to our own Department of State, three of the world's most severe violators of religious freedom are in the Middle East, with Afghanistan right next door.

The current level of Islamic fanaticism has not been seen in centuries. What must be kept in mind, however, is that, without human rights, the Middle East has no hope of becoming part of the global economy.

The violence of the area is fueled by the highest military spending in the world! In 1997, Middle Eastern nations spent 7 percent of their gross national product on weapons, as opposed to the world average of 2.5 percent. Armed forces in the region constitute 2.8 percent of the labor force, as compared with 0.8 percent in the rest of the world. Arms constitute 14.5 percent of all Middle East imports, versus just 1 percent worldwide. In the last half-century, the Middle East has been a killing ground of civil wars and territorial conflicts.

Five of the world's most active state sponsors of terrorism are in the Middle East. They are Syria, Libya, Iraq, Iran, and Sudan. The only documented use of chemical weapons in the last generation has been Iraq against Iran, Iran against Iraq, Libya against Chad, and Egypt against North Yemen.

Between wars, the U.S. public tends to relax its attention to potential enemies.

Having thrashed the Iraqis during the Gulf War, Americans have assumed they are unable to reassert themselves, but R. James Woolsey, a former director of the U.S. Central Intelligence Agency under Clinton, thinks we are ignoring a very big problem when we ignore Iraq.

Woolsey says our foreign policy regarding the Middle East had grown so flaccid the White House and State Department had stopped calling Iraq and other hotspots "rogue states" and began referring to them only as "states of concern."

"We know, according to reliable intelligence sources, that Iraq has a ballistic missile program. Worse still, Iraq is only months away from achieving nuclear capability," warns Woolsey.

In the streets of the Middle East, Saddam Hussein is regarded as the new "caliph" to take on the U.S. Woolsey called foreign policy in this area of the world during the Clinton Administration "feckless." This is a good description of the entire eight years Clinton amused himself in the Oval Office.

Don't look to the United Nations for any help.

Kofi Annan, the UN Secretary General, caved into Saddam Hussein during the effort to allow UN weapons inspectors to remain in Iraq. No friends of liberty, both Russia and China have criticized any U.S. effort to get tough with Baghdad. Both sell weapons to Middle Eastern nations. The UN has a long history of hostility towards Israel.

The odds are that Saddam is waiting to start a war again and, if he can secure enriched uranium, he may have the nuclear option to back up his threats. Does anyone recall who knocked out the construction of a nuclear facility in Iraq, long before the Gulf War? It was Israel. Probably doing for the West what we could not openly do for ourselves. It is Israel that is the West's foot in the door in the Middle East and it is hated for that.

The point I would make is that, even if there were *no* Israel, the U.S. would still need to exercise our power in the Middle East. We simply depend on their oil. Without their oil, we would dismiss the Middle East as we dismiss the entire continent of Africa. I once flew across the country with man who worked in the oil industry. We chatted for much of the flight and, at one point, he shook his head and laughed. "If Americans ever thought that they were running out of oil, they'd be sucking it out of telephone poles."

The simple truth is that right now the U.S. is the only guarantor of peace anywhere. From the coast of China to the deserts of Iraq, it is our power with which despots must reckon. And just as in ancient times, the Middle East is where trouble lives and trouble is exported. Every empire that ever laid claim to it found that out the hard way.

Islam: The Endless Jihad

"The terrorists' directive commands them to kill Christians and Jews, to kill all Americans and make no distinctions among military and civilians, including women and children." So said President Bush in his September 20, 2001 address to Congress and the nation. "I also want to speak tonight directly to Muslims throughout the world. We respect your faith. It's practiced freely by many millions of Americans and by millions more in countries that America counts as friends. Its teachings are good and peaceful, and those who commit evil in the name of Allah blaspheme the name of Allah."

Little in Islam's history, dating back to 610 AD, when Muhammad began preaching, and 622AD, from which Islam dates its calendar, has demonstrated an inclination towards peace and, for decades now, its imams have preached hatred against Israel and the United States. Despite suppressing militant Muslim movements in their own nations, most of the Middle East leadership also contributed to their upkeep and permitted their media to validate their fanaticism.

While Americans are accustomed to expressing ourselves plainly and openly, one of the difficulties to be faced in the days ahead is that the opposite is true of Arab culture. The plain language of the President's address, understood instantly by Americans, is still being parsed by our enemies. In addition, Arabs live with too many bogeyman fantasies about Jews. It clouds their ability to see things as they are. Regrettably, this can be also said of some Christians.

There is, however, a very big difference between Islam and Christianity. Writing in *Jihad in the West: Muslim Conquests from the 7th to the 21st Centuries*, historian Paul Fregosi documented the history of Islam and its attacks upon European nations. "'The sword is the key to heaven and hell,' Muhammad told his followers. Six hundred years earlier, Christ had said, 'He who lives by the sword shall perish by the sword.' It can be said that Muslims who kill are following the commands of Muhammad, but Christians who kill—and there are many—are ignoring the words of Christ." Therein, wrote Fregosi, "perhaps lies one of the basic philosophical differences, as well as one of the basic ethical differences, between Islam and Christianity."

To ignore these differences—and they exist between Islam and all other religions—is to ignore a terrible truth, one that has been articulated by the leaders of Islam since its beginning. The late Ayatollah Khomeini, whose Islamic revolution overthrew the Shah of Iran, is a saint to millions of Muslims around the world. This is what he said of Jihad: "It means the conquest of non-Muslim territory. The domination of Koranic Law from one end of the earth to the other is…the final goal…of this war of conquest."

Fregosi characterized Jihad as "essentially *a permanent state of hostility* that Islam maintains against the rest of the world." Many other historians have seen Islam in this light as well. Bat Yeor's *The Decline of Eastern Christianity* identifies Jihad as "a religious obligation. It forms part of the duties that the believer must fulfill; it is Islam's normal path to expansion." In this respect, Jihad is what Christians would call a sacrament; it is a religious duty that Muslim's must perform if called upon.

In February 1998, Osama bin Laden issued the following order: "Kill Americans." On September 25, 2001, in a statement to the people of Pakistan, he said, "We ask God to make us defeat the infidels and the oppressors and to crush the new Jewish-Christian crusader campaign on the land of Pakistan and Afghanistan." That's worth repeating: "the new Jewish-Christian crusader campaign." Not the American campaign or the British campaign, but one he identified totally in terms of Christianity and Judaism.

For all those loathsome liberals, intellectuals, and Hollywood types who want to blame the attack on America, this is what syndicated columnist Charles Krauthammer had to say, "America conducted three wars in the 1990s. The Gulf War saved the Kuwaiti people from Saddam. American intervention in the Balkans saved Bosnia. And then we saved Kosovo from Serbia. What do these three military campaigns have in common? In every one we saved a Muslim people. And then there was Somalia, a military operation of unadulterated altruism. Its sole purpose was to save the starving people of Somalia. Muslims all."

Americans and others around the world must now consider how we are going to deal with both militant Muslims and the great, largely silent majority of Muslim faithful. Since the early 1980's, except when provoked, America has largely "turned the other cheek," but I respectfully suggest this is no longer an option and this poses some very difficult questions and issues for everyone.

The Kalima, the central prayer of Islam says, "There is no God but Allah and Muhammad is His Prophet." This recitation, said daily by Muslims, is a proclamation of his or her faith in Islam. It can also be interpreted to be a declaration that all other religions are false. By comparison, the central prayer of Judaism is "Hear Oh Israel, the Lord, my God, the Lord is one." It simply declares the singularity of God.

Americans are being urged to avoid giving offense to Muslim citizens. This is a nation that prides itself on its tolerance for all religions. Our Constitution extends protection to the free practice of religion and says in the First Amendment of the Bill of Rights, "Congress shall make no law respecting an establishment of religion," but in Muslim nations around the world, the practice of any religion other than Islam is forbidden, often on pain of death.

A major campaign by U.S. Muslim organizations is being waged to convince Americans that Muslim Americans are loyal. Daniel Pipes, one of the nation's leading authorities on Muslims and Islam, has written that many of these organizations are saying one thing in public and another in private.

For example, American Muslims for Jerusalem publicly emphasizes "the profound attachment Muslims have to Jerusalem" and calls it a symbol of "religious tolerance and dialogue." In a November 1999 fundraiser, however, AMJ speakers, Nihad Awad and Abduraham Alamoudi, reportedly "vied with each other in verbally assaulting the State of Israel and American Jews. In particular, they spun an elaborate conspiracy theory about Jewish control of the United States and Zionist brainwashing of American Christians," noted Pipes.

Pipes has warned for years against "the covert radicalism of American Muslim organizations," suggesting that "Government and corporate policymakers should not meet with them. The media should not quote them as authorities. Immigration officials should study closely whom they invite from abroad. Religious leaders should exclude them from ecumenical events."

American Muslims and surely all others around the world are faced with a profound spiritual decision. Can they break with sacramental ties to a religion that is based upon an unending Jihad against all other religions? Other major religions have evolved over the centuries. Only Islam appears resistant to any change. The President has taken the lead, inviting American Muslims to participate fully in the mainstream of our national community. He is a Born Again Christian and, as such, a man who takes forgiveness and redemption very seriously. The rest of us can only pray that American Muslims take the hand extended to them and grasp it firmly.

For my part, despite the rhetoric in high places, I believe it is folly to think that those in Middle Eastern nations are our "allies" or "friends," no matter how many times our leaders use these terms in the effort to secure their leaders' cooperation to root out the terrorists in their midst. Whether Muslims such as those in Afghanistan are the victims of the so-called fundamentalists among them or whether they are those who danced in the streets of their cities, there is little evidence of anything other than widespread support for the evil that was visited upon the United States on September 11th.

Right now, the reality is that there are Muslim organizations dedicated to the Islamic domination of the world and they don't care who they kill or how many they have to kill in order to achieve it. These organizations include al-Qaeda, Osama bin Laden's organization, spread throughout all the nations of the Middle East and in African nations, as well as those in

Asia and the Pacific Basin. Its cells exist in America and in the United Kingdom as well, and extend into former Soviet republics that include Chechnya, Tajikistan and Uzbekistan.

In the Philippines and Malaysia, there's the Abu Sayyaf group. In Algeria there's the Armed Islamic group. In Egypt there's Al-Gam'a al-Islamiyya and Al-Jihad.

Hamas, Hezbollah, the Popular Front for the Liberation of Palestine, and the Palestinian Liberation Front are groups whose names are familiar to those who have followed the Islamic effort to destroy the nation of Israel and claim its land for Islam. It's claim goes back over 5,000 years, pre-dating both Islam and Christianity. Jews around the world just celebrate Rosh Hashonah, their New Year, whose calendar is 5762.

The United States has had a strange relationship with nations such as Iran, Iraq, Libya, Egypt, the Sudan, Pakistan, and Saudi Arabia. We are extremely dependent on the oil that props up most of their regimes. We have fought wars on their behalf and we have been the target of their scorn. The leaders of almost all these nations have now cut off diplomatic relations with the Taliban. As noted, they have suppressed militant Islamic movements within their own nations, but they have not curbed the ceaseless campaign of hatred against America and Israel.

The President, in his address to Congress, said, "Every nation in every region now has a decision to make: Either you are with us or you are with the terrorists." There has to be a cultural and—yes, spiritual—change within Islam.

For America, the United Kingdom, Europe, the nations of South America, nothing less than the future of Western values, of human progress is at stake. For Buddhists and Hindus, and members of other faiths, Islam must reject its intolerance.

Are there good Muslims in the United States? Yes, of course, just as there are surely millions of Muslims worldwide who personally and privately condemn what is occurring. They must reclaim Islam and they must reform it. For now, however, America is a nation at war with an enemy who killed more than 3,000 of us on a single day. They call it Jihad.

Dying to Kill the "Occupiers"

I confess I can no longer hear the word "Palestinian" without seeing it drip with the blood of their own insanely suicidal killers of ordinary citizens of Israel, infants, men and women, old and young alike. Those who won't strap dynamite to themselves prefer to roll grenades into religious schools where youth are studying their ancient faith or spraying anyone, soldier or non-combatant, with bullets. It is the fact, the presence, of Jewish life that is their enemy.

It is this utter contempt for the lives of Jews that all others must understand as well because includes them. Being a Christian will not protect you, nor being a Hindu, Sikh or Buddhist. Islam is at war with all faiths and all peoples. If the Palestinians can destroy Israel, there is no nation that will be safe from the legions of other Muslims pledged to a holy war, a Jihad.

David Ben Gurion, one of the founders of Israel and its first president, in a proclamation announcing the establishment of Israel, wrote "It is the natural right of the Jewish people, like any other people, to control their own destiny in their sovereign state." As the 1800s came to an end, Jews began to immigrate to Palestine for the purpose of creating a Jewish State. They called it the "Aliya," the return.

In 1921, Winston Churchill, then Britain's colonial secretary, visited Jerusalem, expressing sympathy for the Zionist cause and, a year later, reaffirmed the Balfour Declaration of 1917 that voiced Britain's support for a Jewish State. By the 1930s the war clouds had darkened over Europe. Six million Jews would not escape the fate the Nazis decreed, but, from British administered Palestine, 130,000 Jewish men and women joined the Jewish Brigade to fight side by side against the Nazis.

When the newly established United Nations agreed on November 29, 1947 that a Jewish State should be allowed join the family of nations, 33 countries voted in favor and 13 Arab states voted against the report issued by the UN Special Committee on Palestine. By December, indigenous Arabs began to flee the area allotted to the Jewish State. They were encouraged by neighboring Arab states. They and their descendents would become the oldest body of refugees in history, refused citizenship to this day in the nations to which they had fled.

When the Arab nations attacked, the total population of Jews in Israel was barely 650,000. By contrast, there were 1,200,000 Arabs in what had been Palestine and another 30,000,000 in the surrounding states. The first campaign against the Jews lasted four weeks. In its aftermath, a UN emissary requested Jews and Arabs to renew the truce that had followed. The Arabs refused.

Their descendents, the self-anointed "Palestinians" call the Israelis "occupiers" with every breath. How can you be an occupier in a sovereign land that has existed since May 1948? One whose origin goes back two millennia? How can you be an occupier when you can not dig into the ground of Israel anywhere without unearthing the shards of ancient Israelis, their castoff containers of olives, wines, and, yes, their books.

In a recent speech, Sen. James M. Inhofe (R-OK) spoke of what the area called Palestine was like in the past. He noted that, in 1867, Mark Twain visited the area, later calling it "A desolate country whose soil is rich enough but it given over wholly to weeds. A silent, mournful expanse. We never saw a human being on the whole route. There was hardly a tree or a shrub anywhere. Even the olive and the cactus, those fast friends of a worthless soil, had almost deserted the country."

Where were the so-called "Palestinians" whose supposed descendents cry out their love of the land?

Sen. Inhofe cited a 1913 report by the Palestinian Royal Commission, a British entity, that described the conditions on the coastal plain along the Mediterranean Sea. "The road leading from Gaza to the north was only a summer track, suitable for transport by camels or carts. No orange groves, orchards or vineyards were to be seen until one reached the Yavnev village. Houses were mud. Schools did not exist. The western part toward the sea was almost a desert. The villages in this area were few and thinly populated. Many villages were deserted by their inhabitants."

Where were the "Palestinians" for whom the land is so sacred? Where were those who toiled to turn it into rich groves filled with oranges, grapes, fruits and vegetables to feed people and to export? There were none! This is what the present-day, so-called "Palestinians" are killing Jews for. If there is a flourishing Israel today, if there are acres rich with agricultural abundance, if there is a thriving high tech industry, it is because of the Jews, the Jews, the Jews.

Occupiers? Are the residents of Texas or California "occupiers" of Mexican territory? Are those who live in Florida "occupiers" of Spanish lands? But Jews who live in Israel continue to be called "occupiers" as if they have no right to a place they turned from a desert into a thriving modern nation.

On March 12, UN Secretary-General, Kofi Annan, told Israel to end the "illegal occupation" of Palestinian areas, while calling on the Palestinians to stop killing innocent Jews. In other words, he used the words of the Palestinians to justify telling Israelis they should *not* defend themselves. Meanwhile, the radical Islamic groups, Hamas and Fatah, are competing with each other as to how many Jews they can kill before the next bogus "cease fire."

I recently saw a photo of these would-be Islamic martyrs and was struck by the similarity between them and the members of the Ku Klux Klan. Both show a preference for white hoods and sheets to hide their identity while they go about their dirty work. Look upon me and fear me they are saying, but we do not fear men who are too fearful to show their faces, knowing the evil they adhere to. If there is a Hell, there must surely be a special place for such men.

And, once again, we are hearing about a trade of "land for peace." It is a lethal fraud for the Israelis who, nonetheless, have long been prepared to make this trade. Now the United Nations has gotten into the act proposing, through its Security Council, a separate Palestinian State. The Israelis will no doubt go along with this if it can end the terrorist bloodshed they have long experienced, but there will be no cessation to the insane Islamic desire to take over the Holy Land of Christians and Jews.

Consider the obscenity of Saudis suggesting that, if the Jews will just go back to the tiny area they lived in prior to being attacked in four separate wars by Arabs, then the surrounding nations would respect their right to exist as a nation. The Saudis want Jerusalem to be the capital of a separate Palestinian state. *Jerusalem!* Does anyone believe *anything* a Saudi has to say anymore after their citizens hijacked four commercial jets in order to attack the World Trade Center and the Pentagon? Until his citizenship was taken away, Osama bin Laden was a Saudi.

Are we that stupid? Are we that naïve to think that anything they say is to be trusted? Or, for that matter, anything that the Nobel Peace Prize winner, Yasser Arafat, has to say these days? Do we believe the Iranian ayatollahs when they say they are not protecting high-ranking al Qaeda leaders? Do we believe that Saddam Hussein will not try to supply some demonic Arab madman with a nuclear or biological device to attack a U.S. city?

The United States must change the rules of the game. We must cobble together our cringing, fearful allies in Europe and anywhere else we can find them into a "coalition" that will give us cover to do the job that must be done to protect our nation, their nations, and the future of Western civilization.

We cannot wait for Islam to undergo a Reformation as did Christianity. If its history tell us anything, it is that Islam will never, can never, forsake conquest by the sword. It will threaten the world forever.

The Islaming of Europe

The assassination of Pim Fortuyn, a Dutch politician, an outspoken opponent of immigration in general and Muslims in particular, plus the uproar over the initial success of the French politician, Le Pen, who shared similar views, points out the growing concerns many Europeans have regarding its Muslim population, in particular, and immigrants in general.

It may surprise you to learn that Muslims are the second largest religious group in England after the Anglican and Catholic majorities. There are some two million Muslims in Great Britain. They are not indigenous to England, being largely newcomers from Pakistan, Bangladesh, and India. Others come from Africa, Asia, and even Europe. The Muslims of England are very diverse in many ways, except for their faith in Islam. Increasingly, though, demands have grown for education of Muslim children to reflect their religion, for official recognition of the Islamic faith. Native-born Brits are less than thrilled with their growing numbers and demands.

The vote in France for Le Pen, a candidate with extreme right-wing political views, was generated by a growing concern of ordinary, native-born French men and women regarding their Muslim population and other immigrants. Here again, the fact that some five million Muslims are the second largest religious group in France may come as a surprise; more than half of whom are French citizens. They are largely the result of France's colonial past, especially in the North African region.

Most of the Muslim community in France are from nations called the "Maghreb," Algeria, Morocco, and Tunisia. Others come from Turkey, Senegal, and Mali. Some are converts. Islam has a long history in France. Ironically, the spread of Islam into Europe was ended with their defeat at

Poitiers, France, in 732. It would not be until 1683 when Muslims were defeated near Vienna, that further expansion efforts ended in Europe. Now Muslims merely immigrate to European nations.

France's situation is particularly instructive. Immigration began in earnest in the 1950s, primarily from Maghreb nations. For decades, the religion was largely invisible and Muslims represented the lowest rungs of the economic and social ladder, but, in the 1990s second and third generation French Muslims underwent a re-conversion of sorts, joining the ranks of radical Islam to seek an identity in a society from which they felt excluded.

This is interesting, too, because, twenty years ago, the demand for official recognition of Islam led to the *Charter of Muslim Faith* that defined how a French Muslim could remain faithful to both Islam and France. Today, native French citizens tend to regard Muslims as a danger to their society. The French government, however, has seen integration of Muslims into French society as a wiser path than some form of de facto isolation.

Reportedly, the overwhelming majority of Europe's Muslims see their religion as a moderate one. There are 32.5 million Muslims throughout England, Europe, the Balkans, and the Caucasus. Some are in the process of redefining Islam as people born and bred in Europe. This could be the beginning of a much-needed Reformation within Islam that occurred and redefined Christianity.

Having noted the Muslim defeat outside of Vienna, Austria in 1683, it would not be until 1878 before Muslims appeared in greater numbers as the result of the annexation of Bosnia-Herzegovina and other territories by the Austro-Hungarian Empire. Currently, Muslims are the third largest religion in Austria and growing. Their numbers doubled between 1981 and 1991. These Muslims are largely immigrants and are often political refugees. The bulk are formerly Turkish and citizens of the former Yugoslavia. The recent Balkan wars drove a lot of Muslims to choose Austria as a homeland.

The relationship between Muslim minorities and the State of Austria has been formalized and regulated since 1912 by the Islam Act that officially recognized the religion. It led to the establishment of the Muslim Faith Union in 1979 and Austrians Muslims are taught their faith in public schools with teachers paid by the State. The rise of nationalistic political parties in Austria reflects a concern seen in France. Increasingly, a growing portion of native Austrians are suspicious and fearful of Muslims.

In Poland, chiefly Polish-Lithuanian Tartars, a group estimated between two and three thousand, have lived in that nation for some 600 years. Their small numbers versus the overwhelmingly Catholic Poles has left them largely ignored. Muslims, however, in the post-Soviet Caucasus are a different situation entirely. Islamic fundamentalism has, for example, led Muslim Chechens to use terrorism and war on the Russians to seek a separate and Islamic nation. The Russians have responded to the Chechens in the same fashion as the U.S. has to the Taliban in Afghanistan.

Several former Russian provinces, now independent, but allied republics, have large, if not dominant Muslim populations. These include Azerbaijan, Turkmenistan, Uzbekistan, Tajikistan, Kryghyezstan, and Kazakhstan. Add to this, Albania. The recent Balkan wars were largely religious movements by militant Muslims and, ironically, the U.S. sided with them and against the Serbs. So did the rest of Europe.

So, now, when you say Europe, keep in mind that the nations that compose it are increasingly home to a growing population of Muslims. Wherever a population of Muslims gains in numbers, they begin to demand autonomy or a change in the governmental structure to reflect Islamic law.

Other than Turkey, you cannot name a single Islamic nation that is a democracy. An elite military in Turkey have maintained its secular government since the days of Ataturk, the man who turned Turkey into a modern nation. The Islamic demand for something less than democracy is likely to lead to religious conflict in Europe. This is the danger it poses to the entire world.

The Truth About TWA Flight 800

In May 2002, Bill Gertz of *The Washington Times* reported that the U.S. government had alerted airlines and law enforcement agencies that Islamic terrorists had smuggled shoulder-fired anti-aircraft missiles into the United States.

Classified intelligence reports identified them as Russian-made SA-

7 surface-to-air missiles or the U.S.-made Stinger anti-aircraft missiles obtained covertly from Afghanistan. The SA-7s have a range of more than three miles and can hit aircraft flying at 13,000 feet. Stingers can hit aircraft flying at 10,000 feet and five miles away.

Actually, this was not a "scoop" because, in an August 25, 1996 *London Times* article, readers learned that "U.S. officials are investigating reports that Islamic terrorists have smuggled Stinger ground-to-air missiles into the United States from Pakistan. Senior Iranian sources close to the fundamentalists regime in Tehran claims this weekend that the TWA flight 800 was shot …by one of these shoulder-fired Stingers of the type used by Islamic guerrillas during the Afghanistan war."

In his book, *Sword of Islam*, author John F. Murphy, Jr., wrote that "The *Times* identified the terrorists as belonging to the Gama'at al-Islamiya, the Egyptian group lead by Sheik Omar Abdul Rahman." U.S. authorities called him the ringleader of the 1993 bombing of the World Trade Center and he was convicted with nine followers in October 1995 of conspiring to blow up the Lincoln Tunnel along with other New York City landmarks. The takedown of TWA 800 was, in all likelihood, just a test for a more dramatic attack.

The tip-off that TWA was shot down by a missile came when FBI Agent, James Kallstrom announced that all theories were being considered and, in the next breath, ruled out the possibility of a missile. Even radar tracking data showed a fast moving "virgule" or a slash appearing in close proximity to the jet before it exploded. Radar does not lie. More than a hundred eyewitnesses, some with military and flight experience, reported seeing a missile streak toward TWA 800.

My view is that a missile shot down TWA 800 and the U.S. government covered it up for one simple reason. If people knew that they could be shot out of the air on any commercial jet they boarded, the airline industry would suffer a devastating blow similar to what occurred after 9-11. The fact remains, however, that this situation exists today. No flight is safe.

Right now, the terrorists among us have "gone to ground", but most terrorist actions against the U.S. have had a period of years occur between them. One of these days, in separate incidents all around the nation, several commercial jets will be shot down on the same day. Then we will awaken once again to the threat of the enemy within our borders. And, by then, it will once again be too late.

The threat is further complicated by the fact that this nation continues to allow people from nations designated as harboring terrorists to come into the U.S.. We are not talking about a few hundred, but rather a few thousand from Middle Eastern and African nations known to be Islamist sanctuaries and breeding grounds.

Americans continue to recoil from "profiling" these people, but this simply means identifying a potential enemy. Without such an exercise in judgement and common sense, terrorists like Richard Reid, the famed "shoe bomber," a British Muslim, still can get on any plane and come here.

There is far too much soft, fuzzy thinking going on with regard to restricting access to this nation and we shall pay a terrible price in human lives by and by.

A Letter from India: Warning About Pakistan

Writing to me in June, a friend, a young lawyer from Nagur, Central India, said, "It is not inconceivable that Pakistan wouldn't supply nuclear know-how to the Taliban. This could then create a situation where Osama bin Laden (who) wants to get even with the West and bomb a major American city." As we now know, bin Laden had men training to steal commercial airlines to perpetrate the worst attack on mainland America in our history. Sometimes we need to pay a lot more attention to what our friends in foreign nations are trying to tell us.

On September 16th, *The Times of India* reported that gunmen in the city of Agra had shot a ten-year-old boy and left a note warning the government not to support the United States, otherwise, it said, no Hindu would survive. The boy survived. The response of Indian investigative agencies has been to work closely with the FBI, providing detailed maps and information about terrorist training camps inside Afghanistan. India's intelligence gathering agencies maintain voluminous dossiers on Afghan mercenaries who operate in the northern Indian states of Jammu and Kashmir.

Following the attack on America, my friend wrote to say that discussion of the event had "been heating up living rooms all over India. The country is rife with speculation." Unlike some Americans, he has no doubt that Pakistan is no friend of America. While the mainstream media and pundits continue to ridicule George Walker Bush as a dunce, back in June it was reported he intended to visit India early in 2002. As one of his advisors noted, "If we are going to discuss great powers of the future, then we have to discuss India," adding, "We have to get beyond patronizing stuff. We need to get into real substance now."

So, too, Americans should begin to address "real substance" because India has long been threatened by Pakistan on one side and by China on the other. (Imagine living with Canada and Mexico as a constant threat.) India is home to more than one billion people of whom 80 percent are Hindu and 14 percent are Muslim.

India has the fourth largest reserves of coal and is rich in iron, manganese, titanium, diamonds, and natural gas. It is heavily agricultural, but has a large textile industry, as well as those devoted to chemicals, mining, and steel. India produces huge amounts of spices, cotton, and sugar among other economically valuable crops. India is one of the oldest civilizations known to man. It goes back some 5,000 years, as old as the Egyptian civilization and one that outlasted it by millennia.

The British, busy creating an Empire, set their eyes upon this prize. Though it is fashionable to berate it for having been a colonial power, the British did much to modernize India when it ruled from 1757 to 1947. They gave India a constitution in 1935, at which time Muhammad Ali Jinnah lobbied hard for a separate nation of Pakistan, exclusively for the Muslims. Eventually the British partitioned the nation into the dominions of India and Pakistan. After an independence movement led by a Hindu, Mohandas K. Gandhi, the British stood aside and India became a nation in January 1950. This occurred two years after a Muslim had assassinated Gandhi. What followed independence was a massive movement of twelve million Hindu and Muslim refugees crossing borders to avoid the kind of strife and hatred we now see focused on America.

"While in the near term," my Indian friend wrote following the attack, "the U.S. government focuses on getting even with the Taliban, the real terrorists are escaping through the porous border with Pakistan. The terrorists are mostly Arabs and they began fleeing the moment they feared U.S. retaliation." The important factor here to understand is that Pakistan has long been their safe haven. As we have seen on television, the man in the street in Pakistan has been protesting in the street against their government's decision to cooperate with the U.S. For Pakistanis, their real sympathy lies with the terrorists.

My Indian friend believes that, "In the long term, if the U.S. is serious about ending terrorism, Pakistan would have to be taken to task. The United States would have to wage all-out war against Pakistan because, unless that happens, the terrorist training camps would continue to thrive." That said, it is more likely that U.S. leaders will look first to neutralize Iraq with its weapons of mass destruction. And then maybe the U.S. will turn its longer-term attention to Pakistan. "The picture is further complicated by Pakistan's possession of nuclear weapons, courtesy of China."

At this point, if reports can be trusted, the U.S. is ignoring our shared interests with India. Instead, Pakistan has already tried to dictate the composition of a military coalition to deal with Osama bin Laden's Al-Queda terrorist organization, seeking to exclude both Israel and India. Is it not time to stop complying with Muslim demands? Well, yes and no. Afghanistan is about the size of Texas and the armies of great nations have been defeated there. It is wiser to have bases of operation in Pakistan from which to fight.

India is neither governed, nor populated by saints. Part of its problem is that virtually all U.S. aid India receives disappears down a huge rat hole. The Indian government hires, directly and indirectly, about *twenty million people*. That is more than the entire population of Australia and may well be a conservative figure. As a result, its need for foreign aid is constant. This is the typical Socialist answer to unemployment and India is essentially socialist, in addition to having a thriving Communist party as well. It has long established ties with Russia going back to the days of its Soviet government.

India's security is sorely challenged by both Pakistan and Red China. Writing in June, my friend noted that "China has been sponsoring terrorism in our border States on the east. To that end, they have been sponsoring a military junta government in Burma." Little wonder that India plans to spend $95 billion on weapons over the next fifteen years as the result of its very real, justified fears of China's bad intentions. India wants and probably needs the nuclear option in order to deter China's ambitions and to retaliate against Pakistan if attacked. This is why the U.S. policy of non-proliferation makes little sense to the Indian government.

Pakistan is the other major security threat to India. Its defense expenditure is more than twice that of India's in terms of its gross domestic product (6.5 percent) though it has only one-fourth of India's landmass and one-sixth of its coastline. "Pakistan has been sponsoring a radical Islamic movement in the northern state of Kashmir," noted my friend. "More than a million people have left their homes in the past decade. All non-Mohammedan peoples have been eliminated from Kashmir. It is a genocide worse than Bosnia, but the media doesn't report it!"

India has a huge Muslim minority estimated to be at least 170 million. Pakistan has been reportedly spending lots of money to exploit dissatisfaction among this minority and most of it has come from the oil-rich nations of the Middle East. This minority threatens to destabilize India, which is a democracy based on the British model.

On September 16th, an Indian news agency reported "Pakistan is planning to extract maximum financial benefit from its decision to extend its full support to a U.S.-led campaign against international terrorism." A former senior executive, based in New York with Citibank, was appointed Pakistan's finance minister after a military coup in 1999. Shaukat Azis reportedly has said "Clearly, as the relationship (with the U.S.) grows, I am sure the economic ties will grow which could mean better market access, better treatment on debt rescheduling, and more money, both directly and through multilateral institution." In short, he described a shakedown that would make Tony Soprano proud!

Our relationship with Pakistan is odd at best. It had been under a number of U.S. sanctions since 1990 when it became clear it was trying to develop a nuclear weapons capability. In 1998, it carried out a series of nuclear tests and the sanctions were expanded. Already, U.S. sanctions against Pakistan have been lifted to make them more cooperative. Until the 1990's when the Cold War ended, Pakistan had been the third largest recipient of U.S. aid, after Israel and Egypt. Egypt announced last week that its diplomatic ties to Iraq had been upgraded. So much for having "friends" among the Islamic states.

While Americans wait to see how our government will respond to the Islamic jihad being waged against our cities, our people and Western civilization, so too do the millions in India and elsewhere around the world. The Four Horseman of the Apocalypse are loose again in the world. The ancient battle between the forces of good and evil goes on.

Our Defeatist Press

"With the brutal Asian winter approaching and the U.S.-led bombing campaign in Afghanistan progressing more slowly than expected, a growing chorus of voices in the American intelligence and diplomatic communities is predicting that a resolution of the Afghan expedition may fall short of a decisive military victory."

That is the opening paragraph in a Sunday, November 4th front page article by John Hassell, a reporter for the *Star-Ledger*, New Jersey's largest circulation daily and a member of the Newhouse Newspaper chain. The war is barely a month old. The President has repeatedly said that it will take a long time to secure a victory and warned over the weekend against "an instant gratification" war, but the nation's press seems determined to declare defeat.

The *New York Times* had a Sunday article about the Afghan rebels calling them "a reluctant force so far." Seems they don't like to train when it's raining. The article noted that "the fiery zeal that rebel commanders and solders once displayed may be faltering." It took the rebels of the American colonies seven years to defeat the British during the Revolution. It took the Afghans nearly a decade of fighting the Soviets who invaded their nation to defeat them and that required a lot of help from the CIA.

On the front page of Sunday's *Washington Post*, a team of reporters examined "A Deliberate Strategy of Disruption" as the U.S. rounds up and detains 1,147 illegal and native-born Muslims in an effort to deter further acts of terrorism. "When asked directly how many people have been released, Justice Department officials say they are not keeping track."

Suffice it to say, the *Washington Post* article was very sympathetic to the many Muslims being held, but they were not alone. The lead article in the Sunday *Los Angeles Times* was "Isolation, Secrecy Veil Most Jailed in Roundup." The theme was the same. Oh, how sad it was these poor Arabs and others were having to suffer such an inconvenience at a time when Osama bin Laden is calling for the death of all Americans. Another Los Angeles Times page one article was headlined "Palestinian Militant Kills 2 People in Israel." Apparently there are no "terrorists" in Israel, just "militants."

In sunny Florida, readers of the *Miami Herald* were informed that "Winter Impedes Low-Altitude Strikes."

All across the nation, our press is trumpeting a defeatist message, telling us in one story after another that the United States will lose this war against the greatest threat to Western civilization since World War II.

Anyone who watches C-Span as it televises the live press conferences at the Pentagon quickly arrives at the obvious conclusion that the reporters are the biggest bunch of idiots to be gathered in one place for the purpose of learning about the progress of this war. They ask questions of such astounding stupidity they have occasionally stunned the Secretary of Defense into a momentary speechless state. During a showing of night-vision video of Special Forces preparing for a mission, a reporter asked a General what it was they were putting into the bags they were taking with them. He ignored her.

We are being subjected to the ignorance and defeatism of a press that is virtually salivating over every possible indication we will not win the war in the next week or so. We are witnessing a press that clearly has no knowledge of military affairs or strategy, and no confidence that our modern military has learned the lessons of Vietnam and other recent conflicts.

We are being told we are going to lose!

We are going to have to tell them we are not going to lose this war; not in Afghanistan and no where else we bring our power to bear on an Islam intent on imposing its will on us and the rest of the world. We are going to have to write letters of protest to the editors of these newspapers, send them and the other media tons of emails affirming our confidence in our military forces and the people leading them.

The press needs to join this war effort. That does not mean it cannot or should not accurately report its events as they occur. The press needs to inform us who the enemy is and what his intentions are. This is not a civil war in Vietnam. This is not a humanitarian mission in Somalia. This is not some peacekeeping mission in Bosnia. The press is going to have to support our government or it will risk losing everything this nation has fought for since it was founded. There will be no First Amendment if Islam wins this one.

The Future of the Middle East: Making War to Secure Peace

None of us can really know precisely what changes are coming to the Middle East, but everyone knows that change is coming. My crystal ball says that we shall see all the current leadership toppled. Turmoil will exist in the years ahead for every nation of the Middle East. None will emerge the same as it is today and that is a good thing.

The best example of why the militants or fundamentalists will fail is modern Turkey. It carefully separates the civil administration of the nation from the practice of Islam. This division, however, is maintained by its military, trained in the principles set down by Kemal Ataturk, a visionary who brought about the changes that allowed Turkey to became part of the European community. Turkey is the future.

What the leaders of Saudi Arabia, Iraq, Syria, Iran, Libya, Sudan, Algeria, and elsewhere throughout the Gulf region and northern Africa fear most right now is the demand for human rights and the implementation of freedom through representative governments. In short, they fear everything America represents. They are right to fear this because it is coming. The tide of history everywhere has been turning against the despots, the monarchs, the oppressors who cite Allah or Karl Marx as their gods.

The United States, always a revolutionary force for freedom, is now led by people with the will to change history rather than merely react to events. The desultory and indifferent inaction of the Clinton era gave us two colorless Secretaries of State who effected only a simmering status quo. Our fruitless, feckless foreign policy was little more than a series of "photo ops." The result was 9-11.

I predict severe, bloody, and lengthy struggles in the Middle East and elsewhere. This will occur, in part, as the U.S. pro-actively imposes its will in places like Iraq and Somalia. Elsewhere the kings and princes are likely to be overthrown or exiled by their own people. No where is this better understood than in Saudi Arabia. No where has repression been more ruthlessly exercised than in Iraq. It exists, however, everywhere throughout the Middle East.

There is an inherent conflict between Islam and modernity, and progress. This has created the schisms manifesting themselves throughout the Middle East and elsewhere. The religion as it is currently practiced puts its believers in conflict with all non-believers. This is the reason for the bloodshed we read about daily. "There are 123 verses in the Koran about killing and fighting," noted an Islamic fundamentalist in 1994. "Ours is not a passive religion." There is a great need for a moderate, tolerant Islam. I do not see it happening. Islam, the religion of more than a billion people, will pass into history. Not swiftly, but surely.

Imposing change is absolutely vital for the future of the Middle East because it is mired in ignorance and poverty. Little of the oil money reaches the people, nor improves their lives. Government censorship and oppression is the order of the day. However, just as the former Soviet Union fell as people began to glimpse the fruits of real freedom, so too the war in Afghanistan and elsewhere in the region will shine a light where only darkness dwells.

104

War is the great transforming agent of history.

Sometimes it brings freedom as our Revolution did and as our many other wars have been fought to achieve, but sometimes it leads, as World War I did, to Communism in Russia and, as World War II did, to Communism in China. In both cases, there was little that America could have done to have averted these changes. Russia, previously ruled by the despotic Czar, succumbed to a tragic seventy-year history of economic and social failure. China, a land of competing warlords, was taken over by Communists promising a better life. The flame of freedom was suppressed in Tienenmen Square, but it burns secretly in the hearts of many Chinese.

If the nations of the West unite against the true aims of Red China's leaders, Communism will suffer a defeat there as well. So far, however, even the United States has been willing to assist China, thinking foolishly that, if China can experience the commercial success of the West, it will relinquish its Communist ideology. This is naïve and dangerous. Red China intends to expand Communism and its hegemony.

The Bush Administration understands this. That is why the President wants to build a missile shield and that is why, if Communism does not end through internal events, Red China will be the war that your grandchildren will fight. Pray that its end comes sooner than later. China is arming itself for a great and horrific war.

In the Middle East, North Africa and the Pacific Basin, Islamic fundamentalists will fight with the tenacity of men who know their entire world is coming to an end. Islam is a seventh century religion incapable of functioning in the 21st century. Islam is a warrior cult that puts its believers into endless conflict with all non-believers. This is an utterly self-destructive path to history's ash heap of failed ideas.

The lesson to be drawn from the September 11, 2001 attack is that America must act not merely to protect itself domestically, but to pro-actively effect change in those parts of the world that threaten the fulfillment of the Christmas wish for "peace on earth."

Alan Caruba

On My Mind

APOCALYPSE, NOT!

Okay, I have good news and I have bad news. The bad news is that everyone reading this, including you, is going to die. The good news is that *everyone* dies, sooner or later, and that the "average" life expectancy in the United States today is about 76 years.

Born since mid-century? You will probably see a good chunk of the next one. By contrast, if you had been born in 1900, you basically were dead by 43 and, if you were not, everybody wondered why.

Well, actually, they already knew why. You caught a cold. You died. You ate some bad food. You died. Just about any form of labor pretty much killed you off because the concept of "energy saving machines" didn't catch on until about halfway into the century. In the summer, you sweated like a pig because there was no air conditioning. In the winter you froze unless you had a big pile of coal stacked up in the basement or behind the house. If you were a woman, you were lucky to survive giving birth and, if you were a man, you were likely to become cannon fodder.

Just about everything and anything could and did kill you in "the Good Old Days." Just recently, the folks in New York were astonished to discover that teensy-weensy mosquitoes could kill them. In the old days, the notion of spraying a pesticide was like very new. It didn't catch on until after WWII, but then Rachel Carson came along and DDT was history. Now the EPA is trying to ban anything that might keep you alive.

107

Flies? They were everywhere. In restaurants, in the meat market, flying around the shop where you picked out the evening's chicken, then waited for the chicken guy to throttle it, de-feather it, and wrap it in some oily paper for you. Vegetables were sold by the people that grew them. They were called farmers and had stands on the highway. If something was not in season, you just waited until it was in season.

It was a dirty, inconvenient old world where a visit to a hospital was pretty much a ticket to the graveyard. On the other hand, if you go to a hospital today, your chances of dying from some horrid thing other than the horrid thing you arrived with are still pretty good.

Where I lived, the milk was delivered by a horse-drawn wagon. I swear the damned horse waited until it got to my house before it left its calling card. Horse poop. Multiply that horse poop by lots of other horse poop and you had tons of horse poop and I'm talking the 1940's here! Before the advent of the widespread use of the automobile, flies multiplied so fast in horse poop, disease was commonplace. That's because a fly has no teeth, so it spits on food in order to digest it. Yeah, it spits on it! They are disgusting.

So, thanks to modern medicine, better hygiene, and lots of good food, here we all are at the end of 1999, living longer, healthier lives than ever before in history and what are we told, day in and day out? YOU ARE GOING TO DIE! You can't open the newspaper, read a magazine, or, worst of all, turn on the television without the incessant message. YOU ARE GOING TO DIE! The air is polluted and you shouldn't breathe it. The tap water is full of terrible pollutants. Don't drink it. This is, of course, nonsense, but that doesn't stop the EPA and others from lying about it.

You're told that everything you eat is going to kill you. Hamburgers. Mexican food. Chinese food. Soda. Barbecued ribs. Too much fiber. Not enough fiber. Anything that tastes GOOD. It doesn't matter. Food will kill you. You're eating too much food. You're not eating enough food. You're eating the wrong food. You should eat Yogurt. You should avoid dairy foods. Coffee is on and off the death list so often nobody pays attention any more. And the latest, your veggies and fruits are the result of genetically modified seeds that, guess what, actually allow farmers to grow more stuff on less land. This is a good thing, but you wouldn't know it from the way the press reports on it.

And smoke? Drink? Forget it! They're passing laws to keep you from lighting up anywhere. Drink? You're a social pariah for having a beer or belting back a couple of Jack Daniels. So what if people want to smoke and die early? We've got six billion other people taking up space and that has got to be like way too many! More people should be encouraged to smoke.

Why are there so many people? Because we are *not* dying off like we used to in the Good Old Days. We are all living to become incredibly old people with really bad attitudes. We're doing this in the U.S. and around the world. The do-gooders who want to tell us how to live our lives are very distressed that we insist on eating every day, have already decided how much water you can use to flush the toilet, and wish you just wouldn't drive anywhere.

So you're thinking, hell, global warming is going to kill us anyway, right? WRONG! There is no global warming. That's right. The earth's average temperature hasn't warmed in 50 years. Surprise! Didn't read about this in the newspaper? Don't expect to. Those morons just print any piece of scary garbage the Greens hand them. There's more bad science in your daily newspaper and on television than in some Dark Ages commentary on demons, witches, and their pet cats.

Oh yes, when it comes to pets of any kind, there are the Animal Rights lunatics who (1) don't want you to hunt or fish, (2) consume meat of any kind, and (3) own a dog or cat. Parakeets and gerbils are off limits, too. These nutcases are trying to establish legal rights for Fido and Tabby so they can sue you. As to the animals roaming around in the wild, well, the "experts" are convinced they're all going extinct. Tell that to any suburbanite who no longer has to go to the zoo because they have a herd of deer in their backyard, can find a black bear hibernating under the porch, can't get the morning mail without tripping over a coyote, or play a round of golf without wading through a gaggle of geese. Coming to your patio soon, condors.

What about those hurricanes and earthquakes? More of them, right? WRONG. There isn't any increased hurricane or earthquake activity worldwide. Not that there isn't a whole lot of shaking going on, but it's about the same as it's always been. Major asteroid or comet on the way? If there is, you won't know about until it's too late and there won't be anything you or anybody else can do about, despite all those great special effects movies about blowing them up or diverting them. The Universe doesn't give a damn about you, pal! Nor does Mother Nature who spends most of her time kicking butt with floods, forest fires, blizzards, tornadoes, and other fun "weather events."

Then, of course, there's the "Y2K" bug that will bring all of society to a stop when they flip the switch on the big ball in Times Square. Not happening. Not going to happen. Another big fat lie and you're stuck with a year's worth of military ready-to-eat crappola.

So, as the new millennium dawns, bear in mind, it's just another day. That's it. Throw out the 1999 calendar. Tack the 2000 calendar on the wall and prepare to live a very long life. The Apocalypse has been cancelled.

The High Cost of Saving The World

A Few Things You'll Have To Do Without

You may want to save the Earth, but here's a list of just a few things you should be prepared to do without. The list was prepared by the National Anxiety Center based on programs proposed by various environmental and animal rights groups. It is far from inclusive, listing only a few items whose ban has been proposed over the years or that are deemed unacceptable for a "sustainable" environment:

No more than one child per couple

No disposable diapers

No air conditioning

No automobiles

No pesticides

No herbicides

No power lawn mowers

No snowmobiles

No personal water vehicles

No plastic IV bottles

No plastic toys

No plastic packaging

No new homes

No perfumes

No chlorine

No air travel

No meat

No fish

No zoos

No rodeos

No circuses

No pets

No hunting

No fishing

No camping

No hiking

No mining

No logging

No oil extraction

No nuclear energy

No synthetic fibers

No leather

No furs

No guns

No genetically modified seeds

Primary on the list of things the Greens and Animal Rights advocates want banned are corporations and the concept of national sovereignty. At one point or other, the banning of everything listed above and much more has been proposed to "save the earth."

Columnist Says:
Second Amendment Should Go

He Should Be Worried About the 1st Amendment
(September 1999)

"When will the carnage end?" asked Walter Shapiro, the "Hype & Glory" columnist for *USA Today*. He was understandably upset because another nutcase gunned down innocents in Fort Worth. Who isn't? "It's high time to gun down the 2nd Amendment" was the headline on his plea to rid America of an Amendment to the Constitution that was so important to the Founding Fathers, they put it in right after the protection of speech, press, and religion.

One definition of a liberal is that they believe the National Rifle Association is bad for defending one portion of the Constitution and the ACLU is good for defending other portions.

It is dangerous to forget the Constitution is one, seamless document; the oldest functioning constitution serving a free people. We've now have had *six* lunatics commit mayhem with guns thus far this year, receiving a great deal of media coverage in the process. Compare that with the millions of law-abiding citizens who own guns and harmed no one. Well, that's *not* news, is it? In States that permit the carrying of concealed weapons, the murder rate is well below that of States that do not.

Ironically, Shapiro and others at *USA Today* should be worried about the First Amendment. The August issue of the *Freedom Forum* reports that "Americans are becoming more accepting of limits on free expression, and that has journalists and First Amendment advocates worried."

A survey conducted for the First Amendment Center found that 53 percent of respondents said the press has *too much freedom*. Thirty-two percent said newspapers *should get government approval* for certain stories before publication. Thirty-six percent said newspapers *should not be allowed to endorse or criticize political candidates*. Welcome to the former Soviet Union!

This kind of thinking reflects a population made docile and dumb as hell! As much as I criticize newspapers and other media, I would not have *any* restrictions placed on them and, come to think of it, neither would the Constitution!

112

The Truth About Smoking:
A Government Extortion Racket

The utter wickedness of the attack on the tobacco industry, the naked grab for a new stream of funding by the states that banded together, claiming that they wanted to reduce the health impacts of smoking in order to offset the costs of Medicare for those affected by the habit, is being exposed for the sham it always was.

It turns out, according to a survey by the Investor Responsibility Research Center, that many of the states that received billions of dollars in the national tobacco settlement, not only are not investing much in campaigns to reduce smoking, but are actually investing in tobacco industry stocks!

The settlement created the "largest new revenue streams in state history" according to the IRRC, insuring that 46 states would receive $206 billion from tobacco companies over the next 25 years as the supposed "reimbursement" for the tobacco-related medical expenses of the Medicare program. Presumably, if you could get fewer people to smoke, that would be a good thing, reducing those expenses, but the reality is that less smoking means less state revenue.

A new study from the Council of State Governments suggests that falling cigarette consumption will result in a 20 percent loss of the income projected. Through 2010, states will get $14 billion less from Big Tobacco. That's the last thing they want!

The settlement was never about getting people to smoke less. It was nothing more than an extortion scheme by the states and the people who end up paying the bill are those who, by their own free choice, want to smoke. It's not about healthier people. It was and is about the MONEY.

If they truly wanted healthier people, the states would have banned tobacco use, just as this nation once banned alcohol, but banning things people want as a lifestyle choice is idiotic. The result of Prohibition was the creation of organized crime syndicates because people wanted to drink. And people want to smoke. Just as people can and do *choose* to stop smoking.

So, governments, having generally overspent their taxpayer's money, simply impose new taxes. In New Jersey, the Governor is contemplating a $1.30 per pack tax! In New York, the tax per pack is $1.50, in Washington it's $1.45, in Connecticut, it's $1.10. And it's all obscene!

Government as a huge extortion racket is, in too many cases, what government has become. Everything requires a license, registration, a waiting period, certification, inspections, and on, and on, and on. This is supposed to be a nation where we have personal liberty, but so long as we are taxed for our free choice of what we want to consume, the smoking, drinking or eating habits we want to pursue, that concept is meaningless.

The one thing the federal government and the States have never contemplated is actually spending less; reducing their budgets so they are not dependent on tobacco industry extortion schemes. This constant need to spend more explains why we are seeing more and more States accepting gambling revenues. Once it was only Nevada. Then it was Nevada and New Jersey. Now gambling will go nationwide because people want to gamble. The income stream for the States is irresistible.

Granted the States need income to function, to provide the services needed by their citizens, but deliberately punishing segments of their population for lighting up a cigarette is as un-American as you can get. In the end, it is all a lie and it is a lie whose purpose is to get money.

Our Failed Congress

(April 15, 2002)

It seems to me that, not since the days that preceded the Civil War, has Congress been so filled with arrogant, ignorant, indolent, and sometimes outright traitorous poltroons bent upon the destruction of this great nation and the Constitution that is supposed to be the highest law of the land.

Congress is filled with guilt-ridden millionaires who try to buy their way into Heaven by passing endless new social programs this nation cannot afford, absorbing more immigrants than we can assimilate, and doing nothing to guard our porous borders against our enemies.

Congress has sold us out to the United Nations, signing on to endless treaties that suck the lifeblood of our sovereignty, our right to rule ourselves. They have sold out to the secret communists, the self-identified "environmentalists," who sit up nights devising new ways to attack our corporations and other engines of the economy.

There are, in fact, communists among the members of Congress only they call themselves "the progressive caucus." Hanging is too good for them.

It is insane that our government would attack Microsoft and attempt to dismember this huge engine of prosperity and technological superiority.

It is insane for our government to extort billions from the tobacco industry, a legal business, providing a product people should be free to use or not. The taxes imposed on tobacco products are obscene.

It is pure folly to seek to disarm Americans at a time when an army of terrorists exist among us. These include not only Islamic Jihadists, but the earth and animal rights terrorists that have attacked university and other laboratories conducting life-saving research. These terrorists attack the development of new housing and other enterprises. They attack a whole range of businesses and have done so with impunity thus far.

Led by Sen. Tom Daschle (D-SD), the Senate Majority Leader, some fifty pieces of legislation are tied up because this one man, with his eye on the November elections, does not want the Bush Administration to have any success at a time when our nation is under attack. He is putting America's energy needs on hold. He is conspiring to insure that the federal court system still doesn't have enough judges to function effectively. He is playing politics with our national security and the ability of our economy to prosper. He is not being merely partisan. He is being traitorous.

It is Congress that has bargained away our property rights, protected by the Fifth Amendment to the Constitution, creating new funding by which the federal government and states can purchase more land from so-called "willing sellers."

Congress that has authorized the acquisition by States of more and more land to be put aside from the use of citizens, whether it be for recreation or the natural resources we need to maintain our economy, or the development of new housing for the millions of new citizens added in the last decade.

It is Congress that is destroying our freedom of speech, guaranteed by the First Amendment, by proscribing the ways we can contribute to the political party of our choice and restricting the right to express opposition to candidates weeks before an election.

It is Congress that is permitting our right to privacy to be eroded as information about us is gathered in vast government data banks, including our private medical information. An IRS and an INS that cannot keep track of how much it has collected or where the illegal aliens among us are living are perfect examples of why such information will only lead to horror stories for individual citizens whose data is incorrect. Imagine not being able to get a new job, buy a car, an airplane ticket, or a home because some government data bank is wrong!

It is Congress that has authorized billions more be spent on a totally failed educational system run entirely out of Washington, DC by teacher's unions that control the Department of Education. We are testing and testing and testing students who are being poorly taught in the first place. We are heaping more and more homework on them. We are demanding they submit to drug testing or be required to take mind-altering drugs because they have been diagnosed as hyperactive. Kids are supposed to be hyperactive. Let them have time to play!

Meanwhile, our hugely bloated government has demonstrated how incapable it is of protecting us against twenty terrorists who destroyed the World Trade Center and attacked the Pentagon. It is incapable of protecting our northern and southern borders against a constant flow of illegal aliens. It is unable to find and deport the estimated millions of illegal immigrants among us.

It is unable to coordinate its intelligence gathering capabilities or to analyze it swiftly enough to take appropriate action. It has under-funded our Coast Guard to protect our many ports. It is unable, after spending untold millions, to stem the flow of illegal drugs into our nation. Its answer to airport security was to federalize still more government workers.

The price we pay for this is to have forty cents or more taken from every single dollar we earn, plus pay many hidden taxes. Most Americans are living on less than half their paychecks. They have little savings and a hospital stay can strip them bare of what savings they have. Millions of Americans are unable to afford medical insurance.

- We now live with a government that demands we eat according to its requirements,

- that we drive cars manufactured according to its standards,

- that we give up our homes when it demands the land on which they are built,

- that we visit our national parks according to its requirements,

- that we forego the mining and drilling for our natural resources because of its demands to "protect" the environment,

- that the proper management of our national forests be ignored, leading year after year to cataclysmic fires,

- that farmers be paid for <u>not</u> growing crops,

- that ranchers be denied grazing rights on federal lands,

- that countless "endangered species" are the reason new housing and other development is not permitted,

- that our infrastructure of roads and bridges erode for lack of funding,

- that a nationalized railroad system, AMTRAK, continue to lose millions of dollars every year,

- that our utilities be forced to pay billions to upgrade their facilities, adding to our monthly energy bills in the name of the environment,

- that we yield our Second Amendment rights to own guns,

- that small business be burdened with bureaucratic demands on who they can hire and fire,

- and that we accept a matrix of United Nations treaties and protocols that are intended to undermine our national sovereignty.

Life in America has become too costly for its middle class and barely sustainable for its poor.

These are very real threats to America and few people, in the wake of 9-11, are paying attention to the erosion of rights that millions of Americans have paid with their lives to protect. The America our Founders envisioned has been turned into a Socialist state by a succession of Congresses that have yielded to the allure of more and more control over our lives.

Losing Our Freedom, Our Property & Our Nation

(May 2002)

It's a trend that keeps demonstrating itself in countless pieces of new legislation being proposed or passed by Congress. Americans are losing the freedoms and the protections of the Constitution. Either through legislation or Executive Orders, we are being herded like so much cattle to the slaughterhouse of total government control over every aspect of our lives.

Sometimes, it is just some seemingly irrational new regulation. In Missouri and adjacent States, if you do not eradicate fescue, a species of grass, you are subject to arrest. It has been banned thanks to former President Bill Clinton's Executive Order 13112 on "Invasive Species." Like so many other chickens coming home to roost from his eight years of assaulting this nation, this Executive Order was intended to fulfill a United Nations Convention on Biological Diversity; one whose ratification was rejected by the U.S. Senate.

There is a need for weed control. Anyone battling a lawn full of dandelions knows that, but EO 13112 goes well beyond weed control. It makes illegal the ownership or production of dogs, cats, cattle, wheat, barley, fescue, and every other plant or animal that is not "native." Anything that came here from somewhere else can be classified as an invasive alien species. It is the law of the land and it is a dagger aimed at farming, ranching, and the ownership of all private property. As always, the environment is used as a weapon to attack the economy and fundamental Constitutional rights.

A recent Democratically controlled session of the Senate Environment and Public Works Committee met in complete secrecy in order to vote out (S-975) The Community Character Act. Led by Sen. James Jeffords, this act would give the federal government the right to impose its decision over those of every single local zoning board in America. Nothing in the Constitution authorizes or permits such federal power.

The Tenth Amendment specifically says "The powers not delegated to the United States by the Constitution, nor prohibited by it to the States, are reserved to the States respectively, or to the people."

You may think you live in the "land of the brave and the home of the free," but the America in which you actually live denies you the right to own and bear arms under the Second Amendment, seeking with more than 20,000 laws to proscribe that right.

The recently passed, so-called Campaign Reform Act, the McCain-Feingold bill, puts limits the free speech of individuals and organizations that want to protest the views of candidates, thirty to sixty days prior to an election. In short, it outlaws political speech by all groups, whether it's the National Rifle Association or the National Wildlife Association.

The First Amendment says, "Congress shall make no law respecting an establishment of religion, or prohibiting the free exercise thereof; or abridging the freedom of speech, or of the press, or the right of the people peaceably to assemble, and to petition the Government for a redress of grievances." If you break this new law, you can end up in a federal prison for five years and have to pay a fine of $25,000. Welcome to Nazi America.

There is a push to create a National ID Card for every American. Rep. James P. Moran and Rep. Thomas M. Davis have introduced legislation for this. The Fourth Amendment states that it is "The right of the people to be secure in their persons, houses, papers and effects, against unreasonable searches and seizures, shall not be violated." A National ID Card is a total invasion of the privacy of every citizen. It is the hallmark of totalitarian societies.

In these and too many other ways, elected Senators and Representatives, often with the approval of the White House, are slowly destroying the Constitution and turning this nation into a place where every single piece of information about you will be in national data banks and available to any bureaucrat or elected official that wants access to it. From the day you are born and issued a Social Security number, everything about you will be stored somewhere by Big Brother.

Why aren't Americans up in arms over these intrusions? In part, it is because most have passed through an education system that was taken over in the 1960s by the federal government and which deliberately "dumbs down" the students based on a system developed originally in the former Soviet Union. As they pass through it, it either renders them ignorant of basic skills or, for those who do master them anyway, it inculcates attitudes that harm our society. It is no accident that many schools have begun to resemble minimum-security prisons.

The other element of why Americans express so little concern is the

119

fact that the news media does little to explain the threats to freedom that issue forth from Congress on a daily basis.

Half the registered voters in America stayed home during the last national election. Very nearly half the voters wanted Al Gore to be President. Most of these people live within fifty miles of the East or West Coast. The other half live spread out in the "fly-over" States that provide the bulk of the food we eat, the minerals from which everything we use are manufactured, and much of the energy to power our homes and businesses. These people voted for George W. Bush.

Strangely, though, it was Republican President Bush who signed the Campaign Finance Reform Act; who pushed through a $49 billion education bill that imposes endless testing of students; who advocates granting amnesty to still more millions of illegal aliens. None of this even vaguely begins to reflect the views of those who voted for him.

Lastly, there is the vast matrix of United Nations treaties, conventions and protocols to which the U.S. is a signatory and, therefore, subject to mandates which, more often as not, run contrary to the best interests of our nation. The Bush Administration just publicly rejected the UN International Criminal Court that claims to supercede the U.S. Constitution. The U.S. needs to totally withdraw from the UN.

Home of the free? I don't think so.

The Missing Towers

One gets a very strange feeling as they drive the looping curve of road that leads to the entrance of the Lincoln Tunnel from the New Jersey side. From here, particularly when the traffic was going slow, you could always look over to your left and see the whole of lower Manhattan laid out in all its splendor.

These days, one searches for the two gleaming towers that dominated the tip of the island. Surely it is a dream. Surely, this time they will be there. They are not.

With every September 11th I will be thinking we should build those same two towers again.

I keep thinking of lunches and dinners in Windows on the World, the splendid restaurant that topped out one of the towers and, from which, walking the full perimeter of the floor, one could look out at the extraordinary urban landscape that is New York City and its boroughs, and across the river, New Jersey. Down below, one could see the Statue of Liberty, looking very tiny in the harbor.

It makes me angry.

It makes me angry to think that two planes, filled with innocent people, were turned into flying bombs that literally decimated these two great structures, these monuments to the economic vitality of this nation.

I want those towers back!

Forget about the new designs. They have already been dismissed and an international search is on for still more. I say, take out the architectural plans for the Twin Towers and rebuild them! Tell the crazed Islamists that they did not achieve anything and will not achieve anything. They have signed the death warrant for fanatical, fundamentalist Islam.

Many years ago, I visited the Arizona Memorial in Pearl Harbor. I was a child when the Japanese sneak attack awoke a sleeping nation, an isolationist nation, to the reality that it had real enemies. Ironically, the boat I took to get out to the site was filled mostly with Japanese tourists. What struck me, once we got there, was that they would pause to pray in front of the names of those who died that day, December 7, 1941, "a day that will live in infamy."

The Arizona Memorial is a place of silence broken only by the waters that lap at the twisted, rusting metal of the ship below and the beautiful arching structure above.

I want the new Twin Towers to be a bustling, noisy place, filled with people coming and going. Most will have been born after 9-11 and perhaps some will pause to look at a wall filled with the names of the more than 2,800 who died there on a long ago day in 2001.

I want the Towers back! I want them because this is America and we will *not* be defeated.

Alan Caruba

About the Author

The one word to describe Alan Caruba is "writer." In one fashion or another, from his days as a student at the University of Miami, service in the U.S. Army, as a city editor of weeklies, a daily newspaper reporter, a veteran book reviewer, and as a freelance professional, he has earned his daily bread with the written word.

In his sixth decade of life, he has accumulated the usual credentials of newspaper and magazine articles, and books in the course of a career that has also included recognition as a leading public relations counselor.

He has received many awards for his work and enjoys membership in prestigious organizations that include the American Society of Journalists and Authors, the Society of Professional Journalists, the National Association of Science Writers, and as a charter member of the National Book Critics Circle.

He also gained a measure of fame as the founder, in 1984, of The Boring Institute ©, a media spoof of over-hyped celebrities, films, television, sports and other aspects of our culture. Today, the Institute has evolved into a clearinghouse for information about the impact of boredom on individuals and society.

In 1990, he founded The National Anxiety Center © as a clearinghouse for information about "scare campaigns" whose purpose it is to influence public opinion and policy. He refers to this as "the anxiety industry", constantly claiming that "everything you eat, drink and breath will kill you."

Over the years, between the Institute and Center, Caruba has become a

Alan Caruba

frequent guest on radio and television as the result of his unique expertise and is a popular public speaker as well.

Index

Quantity Discounts

Warning Signs

Give a copy to everyone you know!

Now is the time to get this book into the hands of every American. Order 25, 50, or 100 copies.

Send them to your friends.
Give them to business associates.
Mail one to everyone you know.

Discount Schedule

1 copy:	**$15**
5 copies:	**$67**
10 copies:	**$120**
25 copies:	**$250**
50 copies:	**$425**
100 copies:	**$800**
500 copies:	**$3,750**

ORDER YOURS TODAY!
call: (425) 454-7009
or use the coupon below

Merril Press
P.O. Box 1682
Bellevue, WA 98009

Please send me _____ copies of **Warning Signs**.

Enclosed is a check or money order
in the amount of $_____.

Please charge my: ☐ VISA   ☐ MasterCard
Card Number: _____
Expires: _____
Print Name: _____
Street: _____
City: _____ State: _____
Phone: (_____) _____ - _____

Quantity Discounts

Warning Signs

Give a copy to everyone you know!

Now is the time to get this book into the hands of every American. Order 25, 50, or 100 copies.

Send them to your friends.
Give them to business associates.
Mail one to everyone you know.

Discount Schedule

1 copy:	**$15**
5 copies:	**$67**
10 copies:	**$120**
25 copies:	**$250**
50 copies:	**$425**
100 copies:	**$800**
500 copies:	**$3,750**

ORDER YOURS TODAY!
call: (425) 454-7009
or use the coupon below

Merril Press
P.O. Box 1682
Bellevue, WA 98009

Please send me _____ copies of **Warning Signs**.

Enclosed is a check or money order
in the amount of $_____.

Please charge my: ☐ VISA   ☐ MasterCard
Card Number: _____
Expires: _____
Print Name: _____
Street: _____
City: _____ State: _____
Phone: (_____)_____-_____